Also by John Sellers

Perfect From Now On: How Indie Rock Saved My Life

THE OLD MAN
AND THE SWAMP

A TRUE STORY ABOUT MY WEIRD DAD, A BUNCH OF SNAKES, AND ONE RIDICULOUS ROAD TRIP

John Sellers

SIMON & SCHUSTER PAPERBACKS
New York   London   Toronto   Sydney

Simon & Schuster Paperbacks
A Division of Simon & Schuster, Inc.
1230 Avenue of the Americas
New York, NY 10020

First Simon & Schuster trade paperback edition May 2011

For information about special discounts for bulk purchases,
please contact Simon & Schuster Special Sales at
1-866-506-1949 or business@simonandschuster.com.

The Simon & Schuster Speakers Bureau can bring authors
to your live event. For more information or to book an event,
contact the Simon & Schuster Speakers Bureau at
1-866-248-3049 or visit our website at www.simonspeakers.com.

Note: The names and identifying characteristics of some
of the individuals featured in this book have been changed
to protect their privacy. In addition, the timeline of some events
has been compressed.

A small part of this book originally appeared in *The Believer*.

Designed by Esther Paradelo

Manufactured in the United States of America

10 9 8 7 6 5 4 3 2 1

Library of Congress Cataloging-in-Publication Data is available.

ISBN 978-1-4165-8871-9
ISBN 978-1-4165-9246-4 (ebook)

For Megan, of course—and George

PROLOGUE

Many people have called me a couch potato, but I don't buy it.

The phrase is too geographically limiting, for one thing. "Couch potato" says nothing about the many hours I spend awake in bed each week contemplating crossword puzzles, marveling at the effortless way my wife is able to rise daily at precisely 7:03 a.m., and guiltily gorging on reality shows that focus on people with no special qualities aside from an overwhelming desire to be momentarily famous. The term doesn't factor in the regular procrastinatory marathon computer sessions during which I check the lineups of my three fantasy baseball squads or track down arcane facts about 1980s sitcoms while swiveling obsessively in my desk chair. And while I do of course lounge frequently on my actual couch doing all manner of spudlike things, the futon in my office gets equal usage. "Furniture potato" would be more like it.

Further implied by the expression is that I must look, well, potato-y. Not true. When last I dared to check myself out in a full-length mirror, I glimpsed a gangly physique that was neither ovoid nor pointy in parts—more asparagus than anything in the tuber family. My head didn't sport googly plastic eyes, a huge plastic nose, or oversize plastic ears. At least not plastic ones.

But I admit that there must be plenty of couch potatoes who look nothing like Mr. or Mrs. Potato Head, and some of them may even resemble yours truly, a man an angry former girlfriend once described as "JFK Jr. after a bad couple of years." So go ahead and call me what you want. I mean, certainly I am partial to inactivity, the identifying characteristic of couch potatoes around the globe. Or maybe it's not so much inactivity that I'm prone to as it is in*doors* activity—it does actually require some physical exertion to press all of those buttons on a video-game controller. I realize that this will make me sound pathetic to even the most pear-shaped of adventurers, but unless it involves an athletic field, a questing literary character, or something showing on an IMAX screen, I don't care much for the outdoors. I never have. That's not to suggest that I wish nature any harm or that I don't appreciate it. I am very much on the side of the good men and women striving to preserve our forests, wildlife, bodies of water, and other precious natural resources. I feel outrage and sadness whenever I hear about an oil spill, a corporate land grab, a smog-billowing factory, or the extinction of a species, particularly one wiped out to satisfy the demands of the senseless aphrodisiac and SUV markets. I share basic sentiments about nature and our environment with every other thoughtful human being on the planet, namely that there's some amazing stuff to be found out there (e.g., geysers and narwhals) and that much of it is mesmerizingly awesome (ditto). It's just that I happen to think about these things while chilling out in a La-Z-Boy surrounded by bags of Funyuns.

Frankly, the outdoors has always seemed unnecessarily daunting. The lack of climate control, the abundance of wide-open spaces with no flat-screen televisions for hundreds of miles, the difficulty of finding toilets or meatball subs at critical moments, the probability of being eaten alive by bugs, sharks, and hippos, the threat of being taken out by rock slides, lightning, and quicksand—who needs any of that? And who can deal with the constant menace of ickiness? You can muck up your shoes in a puddle. You can brush up against fungi. You can walk face-first into spiderwebs. You can encounter horsey smells. You can get dripped on by substances that can only be described as *goo*. You can be assailed by rats, gnats, and cheerful hikers who haven't showered for days. You can step in dog feces—or, worse, *human* feces. Almost everything I've ever experienced in the out-of-doors has made me want to come back to the in of them.

So as you can imagine, spending three straight days in the swamps of southern Michigan would not be something I'd regard as a good time. Especially if such an excursion also involved my dad. You might as well throw in a jackhammer to the groin.

Whenever you make a list of the worst situations you might be unlucky enough to find yourself in—and obsessive paranoiacs like me compose lists of this nature roughly twice a month—there's a tendency to include the absurd. *Falsely accused of necrophilia. Forced to attend a Speedo fashion show. Tethered to a wolverine. Tethered to Carrot Top.* But unless you're terminally misfortunate or you have some very interesting substance-abuse issues, these things will never, ever happen to you. Considering them at all is a waste of your God-given list-making abilities.

Indeed, the most airtight list of this kind is filled with scenarios that not only might reasonably happen to you in the future, but with ones that have also repeatedly threatened you in the past. In other words, these are situations that, in one way or another, you've spent much of your life actively trying to avoid.

For me, being subjected to unnecessary alone time with my dad has always ranked at or near the top of this list. So it's difficult to remember why I ever thought that spending multiple consecutive days in his company would be a sensible idea. Nearly three decades after the divorce that allowed my mom, my two brothers, and me to flee the home we shared with him like sanitarium escapees, he is practically the same. He's still broke. He still snores. He still chews noisily. He still dresses inappropriately. He still smokes (only now he occasionally does so while simultaneously wearing as many as five nicotine patches). He's still given to bellowing, often while consuming Franzia boxed wine, "Stick that in your pipe and smoke it!"

Plus, he stutters. Badly. Especially when gooned on Franzia. This would be easier to cope with if, upon being instructed in therapy that mantras and aphorisms can help mitigate difficult speech impediments, he hadn't gleaned many of his safe words from his favorite movies and TV shows. Or if he didn't make use of them quite so frequently.

Take, for example, "Prove it," Jack Palance's deadpan line from the 1953 western *Shane*. Literally anything can and will be followed up with "Prove it."

"Dad, I need a ride to the arcade," you might say.

"Prove it."

"Whoa—this pizza is incredible!"

"Prove it."

"A muskrat gnawed off my left arm on the way home from school, Dad, and a significant amount of blood appears to be squirting out of the stump."

"Prove it."

All of these quirks, as well as any other idiosyncrasy he ever whipped out to frustrate, humiliate, or anger me, are still present and accounted for in the seventy-year-old vintage of Mark Ashley Sellers Jr. Yet for reasons I began to regret almost immediately, or at least strongly reconsider, he and I recently formulated a plan to set off on a three-day trip—the longest stretch of time we would spend alone together since 1986, when we drove straight through a blizzard from Michigan to Washington, D.C., and instead of performing standard-issue fatherly tasks like playing the license plate game or lecturing me about the importance of choosing the right lawnmower, he did unpredictable, border-line-insane things, such as yelling over a Don Henley song, "Semis! Goddamn semis! *Aieeee!*"

This wasn't going to be just any old road trip with my dad into the swamps of southern Michigan, either. I would be heading with my dad into the swamps of southern Michigan to catch snakes.

ONE

I have nothing against snakes, provided that they're hundreds of miles away from me. And I have nothing against my dad, given the same set of conditions. Put them together, up close and personal, and well, you have my childhood.

Growing up during the 1970s and '80s in a suburban area of conservative Grand Rapids, a city of roughly 200,000 residents in western Michigan, I was surrounded by classmates and neighbors who had been sired by pillars of the community. Attorneys. Principals. Accountants. In other words, men who held down stable, respectable jobs. Some had careers that I imagined as being enviable, even fascinating, like that mysterious subset of humans who referred to themselves as consultants. I had no earthly clue what being a consultant entailed, but I liked to imagine that their work involved attaché cases handcuffed to wrists and covert meetings conducted in dark alleys. Or at the very least Lamborghinis. In reality, these consultant fathers were just run-of-the-mill professionals who went to work in suits from JCPenney. They would not have seemed interesting or exotic to anyone else, except maybe to Stinky Pete, the unfortunate kid whose dad emptied septic tanks. But even the sanitation trade seems glamorous when your father is a freelance herpetologist.

Saying that you practice freelance herpetology, of course, is just a flowery alternative to admitting that you're a rarely employed guy who likes snakes. And until he retired a decade ago my dad was indeed poorly compensated for many years to observe snakes in their natural habitats. Yes, snakes—those slithering reptiles fetishized by backwoods religious cultists, considered a go-to protein in hobo cuisine, and famously eradicated from a plane by Samuel L. Jackson. For weeks at a time, my dad would scour forests, fields, and other far-flung locations for these strange beasts, and then return home looking and smelling like the love child of the Swamp Thing and Ted Kaczynski.

What made the emergence of this peculiarity even more surprising is that my dad's first stab at a career was in the Lutheran ministry. Possibly because snakes represent evil throughout the Bible, not to mention Grand Rapids, he worked hard to hide his outward interest in serpents during his three-plus years as an associate pastor. He did have some experience in being secretive where this subject was concerned: According to my mom, she did not become aware of this offbeat passion of his until they were already on their honeymoon, when, without warning during a stroll with her near their beach rental in the Outer Banks of North Carolina, he bolted down a hill to check out a black racer he'd somehow spotted through scrub brush from a distance of more than twenty yards. His snake obsession seldom flared up in the early years of his marriage to my mom and his journey toward pastorhood, and was mostly confined to ministry-related matters, such as the occasional sermon or his seminary thesis about the Fall of Man. But in early 1972, at the age of thirty-one, he abruptly left the church and began inching toward a degree in natural resources management. Nine years later, sporting exceedingly tight bell-bottoms and a Marlboro Man mustache, he entered a profession that would initially net him an annual income of four hundred dollars. That isn't a typo.

When the rare work opportunity did arise, he would take off for long stretches of time, presumably heading south to conduct surveys for various government entities in murky locations that my brothers and I referred to collectively, and always with a groan, as "the swamp," and that my mom, an industrious high school English teacher and unapologetic hater of all things yucky, dubbed her "worst nightmare." These bizarre absences, which generated barely perceptible upticks in income, were difficult for any of us to fathom or condone, especially for a preteen who wanted little to do with being outdoors if it didn't involve walking across a parking lot to enter an arcade. I suppose other boys my age—maybe even those whose dads engaged in the stodgy professions mentioned above—would have killed to have been saddled with a father who never cared if you got ridiculously dirty and who actively encouraged you to consort with creeping, crawling things. But I only ever wished that my dad was halfway as normal as everyone else's seemed to be. Okay, and that I might one day play third base for the Detroit Tigers and hold hands with Erin Gray.

Normal, my dad has never been. His vehicles, always hatchbacks, were visibly stuffed to the ceiling with hoes, tarps, towels, nets, and discarded Carlton cigarette containers, and his bumper sticker read LET'S R.A.P.—REPORT ALL POACHING!, quite a contrast from other parents' sensible sedans and minivans, which were blissfully hoe-free and typically adorned with banners boasting of their children's honor-roll statuses. Well into the 1980s, my dad wore a pair of scandalously tight blue jeans whose disintegration was being held in dubious check by the dozens of gaudy, slogan-bearing patches he had cajoled my mom into sewing over the holes.* He is also notorious for giving impressively disappointing presents. Once, he plunked down a homegrown zucchini on the gift table at a friend's wedding, accompanied by a handwritten note that said, "Behold the fruits of the earth." At the rehearsal dinner thrown the night before my own wedding, he made a big show of presenting my fiancée and me with a king-size Kit Kat, completely worthless "his-and-hers" baseball cards, and a wall calendar that happened to be three years old. My poor mother had it much worse. A partial list of the trifles she received from him at various Christmases during their nineteen-year marriage—and, mind you, each of the following items represents the sum total of what she scored that particular year—would include: absolutely nothing, a Snickers, nothing again, a mood ring, still more nothing, and, two Decembers in a row, a self-help

---

* This includes the one she affixed to a rear pocket in a moment of jealousy that read PAM'S PROPERTY.

book entitled *When I Say No, I Feel Guilty*. When she called him out for merely rewrapping the book he'd given her the previous year, my dad replied, "Ah, but you haven't *read* it yet."

So overwhelming were these peripheral quirks when compared with the demeanors of other fathers that it took me years, decades even, to understand that most people are embarrassed and confused by their parents, no matter how upstanding they might appear on the outside. But as a kid, while I sat in the waiting room at the dentist's office and read in the pages of *Highlights for Children* magazine about the exploits of Goofus and Gallant, those diametrical opposites, it was like being shown important secret messages regarding my dad:

Gallant stocks up on the choicest cuts of meat for the backyard barbecue.

Goofus stores dead blue racers in the freezer, thereby terrorizing anyone contemplating a simple Popsicle.

Gallant teaches his son's Little League team the virtue of good sportsmanship.

Goofus invites an old hippie pal to his son's baseball game and says nothing as his friend clips his toenails in the bleachers.

Gallant safely drives his children to school.

Goofus does all of the following when he spots a snake slithering across the road in front of his car:

1) yells, "Thar!"; 2) slams on the brakes; 3) leaps from the vehicle with the engine still running; 4) barrels into the underbrush in pursuit; 5) disappears for what seems like two days; 6) emerges with the serpent dangling from his grasp; 7) belts out the "He is dangerous!" line from *Jesus Christ Superstar*.

Even more puzzling, these rampant oddities were utterly incongruous with his upbringing. My dad was a self-made weirdo.

Mark Ashley Sellers Jr. was born in Washington, D.C., on September 15, 1940, and raised first in Arlington, Virginia, and then in an affluent section of the nation's capital, the younger child and only son of a prominent attorney and an acquisitive former grade school teacher. His dad was a well-mannered but shrewd Alabama lawyer who had moved north to work as an assistant attorney general under Franklin D. Roosevelt; in the 1940s, after a wartime stint with the Food and Drug Administration, he co-founded a law firm, still in existence more than three decades after his death, specializing in government contracts. He and my grandmother were active in several influential social organizations around D.C., with my grandfather serving a term as president of the Cosmos Club, whose members over the years have included Alexander Graham Bell, Theodore Roosevelt, Nelson Rockefeller, Carl Sagan, and Henry Kissinger. Their two children received educations from elite private schools, and the family employed a gardener, a nanny, and a maid. My dad's sister was even feted with a debutante ball.

You'd never be able to guess any of that if you met my dad today; there isn't a trace of high society in him. But by all accounts, he was different from the rest of his family almost from the start, and not necessarily by choice. At age three, he inexplicably developed the pronounced stutter that continues to plague him, and at five, he contracted polio, which sent him to the hospital for nearly six weeks. These hardships almost certainly formed his lifelong position as a champion of underdogs and outsiders—and it's unfortunately the case that, unable to overcome his pesky stutter, he has effectively been forced to play the role of underdog and outsider himself nearly his entire life (although maybe he didn't need to embrace it quite so energetically!). Despite the bad luck, however, he proved himself to be a fairly typical adolescent, decent at school, sports, making friends, and evading bullies. It wasn't until he joined the diverse student body at the University of North Carolina—where he found drugs, folk music, the protest movement, and God—that he embraced his eccentricities.

In 1962, during the summer before graduation, he hitchhiked around the country, emulating his folk heroes Jack Kerouac and Woody Guthrie, and worked for two weeks as a lumberjack in Idaho. Eventually, he got hired on to service laundry at a lakeside hotel in Yellowstone National Park. Walking directly into this buzz saw was Wittenberg University student Pamela Jill Cheetwood, who had traveled west during the summer between her sophomore and junior years to work as a chambermaid at the same hotel. Born in the small town of Wauseon, Ohio, on September 28, 1942, and raised in nearby Bowling Green, she was the older child and only daughter of a high school football coach turned florist and a quick-witted librarian. A voracious reader, my mom set a goal as a preteen to finish all of the classics before she died—a goal she's still a few titles shy of achieving. She was obedient, brainy, sociable, courteous, and church-going. No matter how hard my brothers and I have pressed her on the topic, she has coughed up no stories of rebellion as a young girl, other than a habit of sneaking the occasional cookie between meals. To three boys hoping to justify frequent shenanigans, this was incredibly disheartening.

Her first act of defiance may very well have been marrying my dad in 1964, after a two-year, long-distance courtship conducted primarily through letters. My dad's were written so eloquently and enigmatically that they caused her to romanticize him as a younger, loopier, stammering version of Henry Fonda, and to say yes when he proposed just before her college graduation. And so, without having spent more than ninety hours in my dad's presence before becoming engaged to him, my mom soon moved east to be near him while he worked on completing a bachelor's degree in the history of religions at George Washington University. She found that summer—during which she planned their Bowling Green wedding without much input from him—to be a difficult one, to put it mildly. Her first week in D.C., while she waited for an apartment share to become available, my mom stayed with my dad's parents, whom she had met only once. The very second night, she was dressed down by my grandmother, whom we all later knew to be a highly opinionated woman with a healthy laugh and a knack for making a mean tomato-and-mayonnaise sandwich, but also a dyed-in-the-wool Southerner with deep-rooted social biases and a gift for making truly harsh backhanded compliments. Because my mom had wished to pay her own expenses and have something edifying to occupy herself with until the wedding ceremony in September, she had made a point of securing a job interview ahead of her arrival—and by doing so, she had become possibly the first person in the history of the universe to apply from a distance of more than five hundred miles for a part-time waitressing position at a Stouffer's, which is now known as a maker of prepared meals found in your grocer's freezer but back then was a chain of affordable, Denny's-style restaurants. She was given a job on the spot. After a long afternoon waiting tables, my mom arrived back at my grandparents' stately brick Georgian house in the northwest part of D.C. and chattily told them how she'd unexpectedly spent her initial day as a resident of the city. By way of response, my grandmother drawled, "In the South, there were two things a nice, young lady would *never* be: a waitress or a nurse." The nice, young lady from Ohio, reduced to tears by her soon-to-be mother-in-law's scorn, quit the following morning.

In those months leading up to the wedding, my mom also began to sense that the man she had agreed to marry was not the one she'd conjured up in her mind as a result of his expertly written letters. One example of this was his inability to feign even the most basic level of chivalrousness. With no friends in the D.C. area, and with no automobile of her own in those years before the Metro opened, my mom was often reliant on my dad and his family for transportation. She had enrolled in the master's program in English literature at Georgetown University and would occasionally study at the Library of Congress with my dad, who was working on his thesis. One evening he left her in the reading room to meet up with "some drug-taking friends," as she recently referred to them, saying he'd be back at closing time to pick her up. After the library locked its doors at 9:30 p.m., she went outside to wait for him on the steps in front of the building. In those days, the neighborhood surrounding the Library of Congress was the kind in which a woman wouldn't want to pass much time without a companion, and after nearly an hour of becoming increasingly convinced that she was going to be kidnapped and sold at auction into the harem of a grotesque sheik, she finally decided she'd had enough. She banged on the locked door of the library and begged a gruff security guard to let her use the house phone to call my dad's parents, who lived clear across town. Mark Sr., who had been getting ready for bed, arrived a half hour later to find my mom in hysterics. Minutes later, his son—my ever thoughtful dad—pulled up in his 1956 Ford sedan, a full ninety minutes after the library had shut its doors. As my mom remembers, "Boy, did your grandfather let him have it." And rightly so.

My mom also told me not long ago that, despite my dad's pedigree, her instincts were yelling at her not to marry him, even on the wedding day. But she decided to go through with it, she said, because 1) she didn't want to disappoint her parents; and 2) "I'm not a quitter." Bad call. While the ceremony itself went down without incident, his idea to go swimming in the hotel pool with his contact lenses still in just an hour before the guests began to arrive at the church should have triggered some alarms. His lenses popped out in the water, and he had naturally forgotten to bring his glasses with him to Bowling Green. As a result, my dad delivered the line that every bride (of Frankenstein) longs to hear from her new husband after exchanging vows: "You looked like some kind of apparition floating down the aisle toward me."

By the time my dad left the clergy, they'd already been through hell—or more accurately, she had. On the long list of things she never bargained for was the continual stream of oddballs he'd invite to stay with them in their cramped two-room studio apartment in New York City, where they had moved in the fall of 1965, so that my dad could enroll in the master's program at Union Theological Seminary. First, there was the jittery college friend with eyes going in two directions. "You couldn't tell if he was looking at you or not when he was talking to you," recalled my mom. Then there was the skinny, homeless panhandler with a Jerry Lewis fixation. This young man, who had initially asked my dad for some pocket change but knew a chump when he saw one, performed a few bits of physical comedy to make my dad chuckle, then trailed alongside him while smacking him liberally with the sympathy card. Unsurprisingly, my dad took pity on him. The wayward youth had already been crashing on a cot in my parents' kitchen for nearly a week, repeatedly extolling the comedic chops of the Patsy, when my mom finally reached her breaking point. For maybe the first time in her adult life, she had entered into that dreaded territory that will lead a small-town girl to take out a marker and some posterboard, scrawl CHARITY BEGINS AT HOME in chunky block letters across it, and hang the sarcastic sign on their front door for her husband to see every time he entered the apartment.

And, of course, later, after they'd relocated to Grand Rapids, there was the mephitic youth pastor with bladder-control issues.

She also spent countless nights sitting home alone during a lonely year in Mineola, on Long Island, waiting for my dad to return from what he called "studying in the city," but what she later learned was in actuality the avoidance of schoolwork by hanging out in the bars and cafés of the East Village. Then there were the exercises prescribed by my dad's unorthodox speech therapist. One necessitated my mom to approach a gentleman she'd never met and engage in friendly conversation with him, all while pretending that she had a violent, lifelong stutter; another, spread out over many months, required my dad to wear outlandish plaid yellow pants and a black Russian fur hat in public. The idea behind the latter exercise was that, by dressing so garishly, he might become desensitized to what other people thought of him. This had a positive effect on my dad's confidence, no doubt, and it definitely explains a lot of things about him, but for my mom it inevitably meant that she would find herself walking down a crowded street with a man dressed in ugly plaid yellow pants and a black Russian fur hat. And this man was her *husband*.

These ordeals, designed in part to bring my parents closer together, had the opposite result. And it's not difficult to imagine why. My mom must have resented being asked to jump through hoops to better understand my dad's stutter when she had obviously already accepted his speech impediment enough to have married him in the first place.

And plenty more resentment built up after he abandoned his respectable, if unremarkable, career in the ministry. He almost immediately started up the practice, two toddler sons and a new mortgage be damned, of taking off on long, budget-busting road trips with or to visit old friends, including the reprobate college buddy who would later clip his toenails at my older brother's Little League game. After my dad returned from that first trip in the spring of 1974—he'd gone to Mardi Gras—he was never quite the same. The man who had earned the nickname "Tank" in college due to his proclivity for overindulging became a regular at bars around Grand Rapids. He also got involved in the counterculture *and* the counter women, and in turn fell away from any semblance of decency, all at a time when my mom, who was searching for a job as a high school English teacher while essentially raising two children by herself, just needed some moral support and financial stability. She requested a trial separation in 1975, and that probably should have been it.

In the months that followed, her mom confided in her that they always wished she'd had the good sense never to marry my dad in the first place (Donna Cheetwood, circa 1976: "He's just not normal."), a sentiment shared by her new friends at the suburban high school at which she'd found employment. My siblings and I are of course relieved that she did marry my dad, and everyone's thankful that they reconciled after being separated for nearly two years, if only because it led to Matt, our little brother, joining the family. But we also suspect that Pamela Cheetwood Sellers would take a marital mulligan if she could. "At first your dad's behavior was funny and cute and amusing," she told me recently. "But that lasted for only about two years. Then my life just became total Bizarro World."

Now, my dad has many good qualities, as well, or this expedition into the swamps of Michigan would have been a kind of forced march. He's uniquely hilarious, for one thing—or more accurately, is himself a unique object of hilarity. My dad's finest attribute may be his ability to laugh heartily at himself, a trait that in turn has helped us deal with his endless string of idiosyncrasies, in part because it has given us the green light to make them and him the butt of countless family jokes, without fear of retribution.

One incident he's still complicit in being razzed about, thirty years later, stems from his nonchalant demeanor during an accident we got into one winter while driving down to Bowling Green, where Thanksgiving dinner was waiting for us at my grandparents' house. A light snowfall had kicked up into a major blizzard, and somewhere outside Ann Arbor my dad ran over a patch of ice. The car skidded out and began to spin toward the ditch in a slow, menacing circle. This may be apocryphal, but his all-too-willing acceptance of this potentially disastrous situation was demonstrated first by removing his hands from the steering wheel, then by picking up the drinking jar at his side, then by taking a carefree swig, then by setting the jar back down, then by lighting a cigarette, then by smoking it down to the filter, then by stubbing it out in the ashtray, then by telling a joke that no one understood, then by adjusting the rearview mirror, then by turning down the radio, then by patting toddler Matt reassuringly on the head, and only then by announcing, "Here we go!" as we careened toward probable death-by-snowbank. Many years later, my dad confided in me that he'd smoked a joint in the bathroom of a service station we'd stopped at a few minutes before the accident, which, in retrospect, makes too much sense.

He allowed us to tease him copiously about a quirk, inherited from his Southern-born parents, of saying "the which?" whenever he misheard or didn't understand something one of us would say, instead of the more logical "what?" or "huh?" So when you caught him off-guard asking him whether he liked Double Stuf Oreos, he would reply, "The which?" Various pronunciations that were the product of his upbringing—such as calling a particular severe weather phenomenon a "hair-a-cane"—also produced punishment-free laughter, as did mockery of his impressive propensity to use up roughly an entire roll of paper towels with every meal.

And of course there was the underpants incident.

In the spring of 1969, my dad started looking for a permanent position in a Lutheran congregation and landed an interview with a church council near York, Pennsylvania. He traveled there alone and stayed overnight with one of the place of worship's most esteemed member families. A few days after he returned to New York City from the interview, my mom opened the mailbox for their apartment near Columbia University and found a manila envelope addressed, almost disdainfully, to "Sellers." Standing in the lobby of their building, she looked inside the package and was surprised to discover that it contained a pair of dirty underwear—my dad's used tighty-whities. No note accompanied the envelope. My mom brought the packet and its questionable contents upstairs and asked my dad why someone might be sending him a pair of underpants. He said that he must have left them in the bed. Sleeping nude, my dad went on to explain, was a habit he'd picked up in childhood; forgetting about his discarded intimates was a chronic condition, as his mother had questioned him more than once about similar packages that had arrived unheralded at their house. Needless to say, my dad didn't get the job. By the time I was old enough to understand how amazing this story was, it was already a thing of legend. And so whenever he received a large parcel of mail and set about to open it, one of us would make a point of asking, "Let me guess, Dad— underpants?"

Best of all, though, he loved games and, just as important, had the patience required to play them with us. From 1978, when my dad quit his post-ministry day job as a city social services administrator to attend classes at Michigan State University, until 1983, when my mom, my brothers, and I moved to a separate residence, there was no activity more entertaining than sitting on the front porch with him at night while he sipped from the Jar of Death. This container, also known as the JOD, was so named for its unusual contents: an admixture of instant coffee, Carnation powdered milk, Diet Coke, and Carlo Rossi Chablis. For hours on end, as he drank contentedly from the JOD and chain-smoked Carltons, we played game after game of APBA, a satisfyingly authentic Major League Baseball simulator involving dice, reference cards, graph paper, and unhealthy amounts of whining and accusation. On the porch we also played rummy and canasta, Battleship and Monopoly, go fish and go, Chinese checkers and regular checkers, Trouble and Risk and Sorry, liar's poker, Uno, Parcheesi, Candy Land, and war. No matter how uncomfortable and messy our lives got elsewhere, the porch was always a kind of paradise—even when my brother Mark invariably let his competitive desire to dominate the world get the better of him when facing certain defeat, and spat on the cards or hurled the dice across the front lawn before stalking off to the kitchen in a rage.

Still, while my dad and I have found plenty of common ground over the years, I've always been keenly aware of the sizable gap between our personal philosophies, even if his had remained something of an enigma to me as I entered my late thirties. What had mystified me most was that he had been approximately that age himself when he'd heeded the call of the wild and essentially started over. He had done so at a stage in life when most adults, myself included, desperately attempt to cling to hard-fought mortgages, dental insurance plans, and cable TV hookups, not to mention significant others and steady paychecks. That baffling thought had led to a belated curiosity about what could have made a man in the prime of his life decide to chuck everything, including his parental duties, to devote his life to an animal that most people consider weird, and probably even gross.

Plus, it had raised a few questions that I didn't have the answers for. Why snakes? Why not a more useful or cuddly species, like cows, chickens, or koalas? Or cats? I love cats! Could there have been something about snakes that I and nearly everyone else in the world—including my wife, whose no-nonsense father is one of the world's foremost experts in postage-meter fraud—were failing to understand? As unappealing as swamps may look to the naked eye, my dad has taught me by example that reptiles and their habitats are worth protecting, and I've always been in support of the conservation movement from the comfort of my well-worn armchair—but maybe I had been missing the point by not getting actively involved in their preservation? Also, since my dad was never going to meet me for a round of golf at the country club and I had been looking to build a stronger relationship with him while I still had the opportunity, how could I have even begun to make that happen without examining his lifelong passion?

As much as I had resisted the notion through the years, the means to finding the answers to all of these questions was clear: I would have to experience firsthand the murky and frightful places in which my dad spent hundreds, if not thousands, of man-hours searching for and tending to his favorite species of reptile, the endangered copperbelly water snake. And to truly comprehend what I was looking at and why it mattered, I would need him to take me there. Also, given his advancing age and health-averse habits (which included regularly taking "knockout" pills and mainlining Hellmann's), and factoring in that encroaching development was continually threatening the stretch of wilderness in southern Michigan where my dad's copperbellies once thrived, we would have to go there sooner, rather than later.

So over e-mail, without thinking much about the many possible terrible repercussions, I had asked if it would be okay if I joined him the next time he ventured into his preferred swamp to search for snakes, something he still tried to do every spring, despite being more than a decade removed from physically taxing survey work. More accurately, I had inquired as to whether I might be able to "tag along," as if he would merely be heading to an Office Max and not into a vermin-infested quagmire that I had long held up as being the worst place on earth, even though I had never once set foot there.

This was how, just three months after that impulsive inquiry—to which my dad replied, "Bonzai! Bocephus! Yeeeeeeehaaaaaa!!!"—I found myself standing outside the Delta Air Lines terminal in Detroit, feeling sick to my stomach and marveling that I'd actually spent money to get there. The round-trip plane ticket from New York had set me back $158.20, a princely sum only when you consider that it had facilitated the previously unthinkable.

In a few hours, I would be expected to enter the swamp for the first time.

TWO

As my dad's two-tone Subaru Outback truckster approached the curb in front of me, he thrust his left hand out his open window and flashed me the peace sign, an anachronistic gesture he made many times when picking me up in front of my junior high school in the 1980s, much to the roaring delight of my friends. Even though only strangers talking on their cell phones or wrestling with their bags could have witnessed him letting this one fly, it was all I could do to ignore the many voices inside my head begging me to pretend not to recognize him. It was a mighty struggle not to start walking, fast, in the direction of Ypsilanti.

Instead, I hopped inside. Immediately I was assailed by a familiar smell—a confluence of hours-old coffee, stamped-out cigarettes, and cheap aftershave lotion (most likely Skin Bracer)—that was the odor of a hundred awkward family outings around Grand Rapids. In many ways, this aroma will always be the olfactory manifestation of the way my brother Mark used to pin me down, grab my arm, and force my own hand to smack repeatedly into my face, while he gleefully taunted, "Why are you hitting yourself? Why are you hitting yourself?" And certainly, to confront myself with the indelible smell again was a form of masochism, yet it was peculiarly comforting to know that though many years have gone by, some things remained the same, even Skin Bracer. Who knew they still made that vile stuff?

Bob Dylan, as expected, was emanating from the Outback's speakers. While my dad unquestionably loves snakes, and, in fact, may be the only Lutheran minister in history to leave his post in order to chase after them, his replacement religion is actually Dylanism. Dylan's music was there to motivate my dad while he prowled for slithering creatures great and small, and it rode shotgun in his Honda Civic as he returned home, often smelling as if he'd poured a bucket containing sewage and cigarette butts over his head to cool off. Nearly every evening at our house he could be counted on to approach his record player and perform the following steps: Pull out [insert Dylan album name here, with a high probability of *Highway 61 Revisited*]. Place on turntable. Drop needle. Commune. Repeat. As frequently as possible, despite pleas for mercy. These liturgical binges could not have wreaked more havoc around us if his copy of *Bringing It All Back Home* had morphed into an F5 tornado.

For day one of our expedition, my dad elected to wear the old T-shirt depicting a scary bald eagle superimposed over a billowing American flag. This shirt should not be confused with the oversize sweatshirt bearing an illustration of a scary timber wolf baying at a full moon, an item of clothing that I would have been willing to wager thousands was stowed somewhere in the mildewy recesses of the Subaru. My dad's face—with its prominent nose, deep-set eyes, and high forehead (clunky, metal-frame glasses and unkempt, graying goatee notwithstanding)—has always resembled the craggy profiles on Mount Rushmore, but it was looking paler and pastier that morning than it had when I'd last seen him at Thanksgiving six months previously. That physiological development, however, might have merely been a by-product of his de facto boycott against his car's air-conditioning feature, which was shut off even on a June day as brutally muggy as this one was shaping up to be. To his old-school Southern-bred constitution, the breeze coming in through the open car window was climate control enough. "It's nature's AC" is how he has always explained it.

As I got situated in the passenger seat in preparation for the hundred-mile drive ahead of us, my dad grinned broadly at me. And what a smile it was. A number of his teeth were newly absent, courtesy, as he had told me in an e-mail a few days before the trip, of a dentist who had yanked them before they could fall out on their own. "Still, I can scare off any intruders or act like an inbred backwoodsman or a bum," he'd written. "I can also look poor, so I get some benefit$ [*sic*] and kicks outta that." I wasn't really sure what those benefits might have been, but I took his word for it. All I knew was that I wouldn't have been taking the loss of my own teeth with such good humor, as such a calamity would surely have meant having to give up Jujyfruits, thereby eliminating all the fun out of going to movie theaters. In any case, a partial was said to be on order and ready for a fitting in July. In the interim, my dad had in his possession some goony false teeth to help him "chawmp" (as he'd put it), but he only wore them to eat, apparently. "Take care of your teeth," his e-mail had concluded. "They're all ya got!"

"Hello, big suh," he said, offering up a limp right hand to shake.

Over the past decade the muscles in his right shoulder had atrophied due to what had been diagnosed as either post-polio syndrome or a severely pinched nerve, and their degeneration had been compounded by my dad's stubborn insistence that physical therapists were no more qualified to treat such infirmities than witch doctors. For all intents and purposes, the arm had become vestigial, like the short forelimbs of a Tyrannosaurus rex are (probably erroneously) said to have been. So, to shake my hand, he had to hold his right wrist with his left hand and lift it toward me. Once in my grasp, his right hand just sat there; I had to do all the work.

"Move my arm," he commanded.

In his prime and even into his fifties, I could never beat my dad at arm wrestling, even during that eleventh-grade weightlifting phase that caused my older brother's friends to refer to me, disparagingly, as Vinny, an allusion to the ogrish, Heisman-winning University of Miami quarterback Vinny Testaverde. Thanks to the malady, my dad's right limb would have moved if I had so much as coughed on it. It was shocking how quickly the once sort-of-mighty had fallen, and it was yet another nettling reminder, like every gray hair on my head, of the evils of the passing of time. But I played my part: I feigned extreme exertion while pretending to tug on his arm and used my best Superman-in-peril voice to say, "Arm . . . won't . . . budge. Must . . . move . . . arm . . ." And then I switched suddenly into He-Man mode and easily jerked his feeble appendage toward me as if it were a refrigerator door. This ritual, which we'd jokingly been performing for nearly two decades, was required to be carried out in this precise order every time we greeted each other.

My dad exited the airport and we hurtled west on I-94 toward Jackson, Michigan, at the breakneck speed of sixty-four miles per hour, six below the posted speed limit and a good ten slower than the soccer moms and stoic farmers whizzing by us in massive SUVs and pickups. Whereas most people strive to get from point A to point B in as little time as possible, my dad has always been primarily concerned with checking out and commenting on the scenery while driving, no matter the effect it might have on his cruising speed. "Haystacks on the horizon," he noted absently as we passed a farm; later, he added, "Storm clouds a-brewing!" His behind-the-wheel dawdling was a consequence of two incongruous habits: 1) driving slowly allowed him to better scope the ground for snakes, even on terminally snake-free highways; and 2) it prevented him from having to worry about attracting the attention of the police, of whom he had developed a chronic paranoia, a residual fear from the twenty-plus years during which he reprehensibly used to drink and drive—and not just in a "dashing home after tying on one too many at the bar" sort of way, as his trusty co-pilot had very often been the wine-infused JOD. Some of his idle observations during our drive—for example, "The meskeets are going to be out today"—would have merited follow-up questions if only he had been making the car go ten miles per hour faster. But it was hard for a guy like me, who considers himself the A. J. Foyt of the Brooklyn-Queens Expressway, to enter into a discussion when I was constantly thinking, "Drive! For the love of God, dude, drive!" despite not being particularly enthusiastic about what was waiting for us at our final destination.

Still, we managed to fall into a conversation about just that. We were heading to what my dad kept referring to as a lakeside cabana in Hillsdale County, an area which, as I knew from pre-trip research, is situated on a boggy stretch of rolling lowlands fifty miles south-by-southwest of Jackson, not far from where Michigan forms a border with Indiana and Ohio. The region is chief among the many Midwestern locations in which my dad, in the 1980s and '90s, conducted low-paying government surveys to track and document healthy, undisturbed clusters of copperbelly water snakes—which, sadly, were no longer healthy or undisturbed.

"There was a tragedy . . ." said my dad, trailing off.

Whenever my dad is confronted by the realization that the slithering animals he spent the majority of his working years observing may be living on borrowed time, despite his many successful efforts to protect them over the past three decades, he gets a bit emotional. And in terms of very real threats facing their habitat—land development, industrial pollution, and a small percentage of unsympathetic Hillsdale residents, such as the litigious folks who made an unsuccessful push to get approval to build a motocross course on protected lands a few years back—he's more than justified in feeling bitter. As we approached Ann Arbor, he told me, with a dismay in his voice that felt somehow contagious, about the aforementioned tragedy, which occurred in the early 1990s. It seemed that an overzealous college professor with a sizable research grant had captured six female copperbellies and had fitted them with experimental radio-tracking devices, not realizing that they were all pregnant. The snakes had reacted negatively to the devices and had died before giving birth, thereby depriving the ecosystem of as many as a hundred copperbelly young per year and causing a trickle-down effect in the vibrancy of the overall population for decades to come.

"That was a major blow," concluded my dad, so solemnly that it was almost as if he was talking about friends or family members. I had always known my dad to be sentimental (as his bimonthly e-mails dissecting how his life has been shaped by the movie *Shane* and the oeuvre of Walter Matthau attest), but his openly emotional display on this topic was still surprising. I briefly wondered if he'd ever given a snake a proper funeral. It wouldn't have shocked me at all, actually. In fact, given his past as a minister, I would have put the odds at fifty-fifty.

Because monitoring these harmless snakes—there is only one venomous species native to my home state, and that's the Eastern massasauga, also known as the Michigan rattler—has been a life's work spent almost entirely in isolation in the pre-Internet age, my dad has the tendency to talk about serpents with a passion not unlike that of a crazy cat lady crowing about her pets. It's worth noting that despite all this chatter, he rarely stutters when discussing snakes. Maybe it's a psychological comfort zone for him. Maybe it's just practice. Or maybe it's a pact with the devil. Either way, as he spoke, the Subaru slowed almost to the velocity of a covered wagon.

"You do know that the speed limit on freeways is now more than fifty-five miles per hour, right?" I asked. "That it's not 1970 anymore?"

"I have a little bit of trouble talking and driving," he admitted, and laughed at my mock annoyance. "I can drive, or I can talk."

"Mush, Malamute, mush!"

The teasing shamed him into setting the cruise control at a more twenty-first century–appropriate sixty-eight miles per hour. With haystacks on the horizon and storm clouds a-brewing, we were positively flying west across southern Michigan. If the cruise control managed to stay engaged, we would make it to Jackson, the halfway point of our drive, within the hour. Then, after stopping there to load up on groceries and supplies, we'd hop on the north-south corridor U.S. Route 127 and head due south for roughly an hour, where country roads were awaiting us for a leisurely zigzag farther west into Hillsdale County—and the swamps within.

As we pushed on along the brain-numbingly flat Interstate 94, I decided that it was finally the right time to hear the story behind my dad's interest in snakes. It was entirely possible that he had divulged this information to me at some point in my childhood, but if he had, I'd either forgotten it or willfully suppressed it. (Probably the latter; like many kids, I beat thoughts of really boring stuff, like algebra and Alexander Haig, into the far reaches of my brain.) But not knowing his snake origin story wasn't really going to get us anywhere. It was like growing up the son of a military veteran and having no clue as to which war your father had served in, or like the son of a billionaire not knowing how his dad had amassed his fortune.

As extraordinary as a discussion of snakes would have been in most households, it was tediously commonplace in ours. It's not as though I was actively uninterested in my dad's consuming passion; it's just that it felt like background noise. So when he'd start nattering on about copperbellies or hognoses or blue racers (something it seemed like he did at least every other day), I'd outwardly pretend to listen. But in my head I'd be ruminating about, say, the Pac-Man pattern that would allow me to get past the fifth key. When we reach a certain age, however, our knee-jerk childhood reactions start to feel as silly as the words "the Pac-Man pattern that would allow me to get past the fifth key." I had, after all, eventually learned to like spinach—although it remained to be seen whether my dad discussing snakes on this trip would be the equivalent of spinach, or the equivalent of Brussels sprouts, a vegetable that I firmly believe should be euthanized. Anyway, it was embarrassing, really, that I had never bothered to commit the tale behind my dad's interest in snakes to memory. And my dad must have been waiting for me—or anyone—to inquire, too, because when I asked him about it he unleashed the story with an almost rehearsed gusto.

Like ninety-nine percent of people on the planet, he had been frightened of and hostile to serpents as a young child—but only, he said, because he had lacked experience with them. His antagonistic attitude toward them began to change to empathy after a family beach vacation on the Chesapeake Bay in 1945. "I was playing with a boy my age—Jimmy, from the cabin next door to ours," said my dad, staring vacantly at the highway ahead of us. "We were building sand castles and other things from sand, which we got from under Jimmy's cabin. There was a path we walked up and down most of the morning to get the sand. Jimmy's mother came out, and insisted we come up on the porch immediately. She pointed out a snake coiled right beside the path we had been using. As I learned, it was a copperhead.

"Jimmy's mother called the main lodge, and a young man came up with a dirt rake. As we watched, he prodded the snake, which moved very quickly toward the thicket between our cottages. He then impaled the snake right behind the head, killing it. And then he held it up in the morning sun.

"In the full morning sunshine, when he held it up, the two-tone orange of that snake was beautiful to me. I can still see how beautiful it was. Here we had passed right by it many times that morning, and it had not tried to bite or harm us." He looked over at me, still seemingly irritated by the injustice six decades later. "That was when I became charmed by snakes."

From that day forward, reptiles that he collected around his family's quiet neighborhood made regular appearances in water basins throughout his house, a habit his decorous parents learned to tolerate in the same fashion that some homeowners are forced to concede that they'll never get rid of the mold in the basement or many dog lovers must make peace with chewed-up slippers.

Like his and everybody else's, my first thoughts about snakes were also negative. Many people around my age have the animator Chuck M. Jones to blame for this. An annual treat as a young boy in those dark days before VCRs, DVD players, and affordable cable television was watching *Rikki-Tikki-Tavi,* the Warner Bros. cartoon artist's brilliant 1975 adaptation of the Rudyard Kipling story. You just knew this program was required viewing because CBS would herald it using the exciting trumpet-and-bongo theme music and spinning, multicolored SPECIAL logo that the network also trotted out before its can't-miss holiday specials starring Charlie Brown, Frosty the Snowman, and Rudolph the Red-nosed Reindeer. In the thrilling cartoon, narrated dramatically by Orson Welles, you quickly learn that Rikki-Tikki-Tavi is a mongoose with a cobra problem. By the end of the half-hour show, after Rikki-Tikki-Tavi dispatches the pair of murderous asps with dexterous resolve, you also are made aware that this mongoose is a complete badass. Throughout, you really have no choice but to root actively against the snakes—this is good versus evil at its most basic level, and those sinister, hissing cobras are totally evil! And when that spunky pet mongoose dives into the snakes' lair after one of the venomous cretins, and our furry hero takes what seems like forever to materialize, and the strangely effeminate bird says, "It's all over with Rikki-Tikki—we must sing his death song," I mean, you almost want to cry. That scene alone was a chief contributor to my irrational childhood belief that all snakes were bastards and deserved to die a slow, horrible death, like Brussels sprouts.

"Movies like that one, and *Snakes on a Plane,* and

Anaconda," said my dad, after listening to me coo nostalgi-
cally in the passenger's seat about *Rikki-Tikki-Tavi,* "have
undone most of my life's work at gaining support and tolerance for snakes from the public." He sighed. And then he
added, with a trace of sarcasm in his voice, but mostly a
genuine sense of confusion, "I guess people would rather be
scared and terrified than happy, excited, and enjoying a great
piece of our national heritage."

He had a point. But while nothing will ever make up
for the factual atrocities committed by *Anaconda,* or by Jon
Voight's attempt at a Paraguayan accent in that 1997 corker
(tagline: WHEN YOU CAN'T BREATHE, YOU CAN'T SCREAM), a
valid counterargument can be made that being scared and
terrified by snakes makes a good number of people happy
and excited, as well, or there wouldn't have been three (increasingly preposterous) sequels.

It's obvious, though, that my dad was right about one
thing: The negative perception of snakes by the general pop-
ulace has been both perpetuated and exacerbated by how
they have been depicted in popular culture and literature.
Off the top of my head, I'm hard-pressed to think of a single
favorable example of snakes in movies, TV shows, books,
or music, unless you count the occasional nature documentary (although those just as often trot out the snakes-as-
scoundrels chestnut) or the horny lyric from Sir Mix-a-Lot's
"Baby Got Back" that goes "My anaconda don't want none/
unless you've got buns, hon." Even the one truly admirable
representation of a snake in pop culture that I've turned up
as I've dug a little deeper has something of a forked history.
Kaa, the wise, three-hundred-year-old python who acts as

mentor, protector, and ally to "man-cub" Mowgli in several stories within Kipling's *The Jungle Book,* has been morphed into a one-dimensional meanie in Disney's popular 1967 animated movie of the same name. With swirling, hypnotic eyes and a ridiculous lisp, this far-more-famous version of Kaa comes across as being as purely evil as the nefarious Nag and Nagaina of Kipling's story "Rikki-Tikki-Tavi" (as well as Chuck M. Jones's faithful cartoon adaptation of it): He's a deceitful character salivating at the mere prospect of consuming Mowgli whole. In the process, he has been turned into yet another snake we are encouraged to hate.

And there are a lot of these sorts of examples, none more superfluous or more memorably named than Sir Hiss, a Kaa look-alike used as a comedic foil in another animated Disney movie, 1973's *Robin Hood.* Sometimes snakes have been cast, in the manner of Nag and Nagaina, as archvillains—menacing, scene-stealing roles that, in another context, might have been played by Rutger Hauer. There's the massive one in *Anaconda,* sure, but also Voldemort's sinister pet viper in the *Harry Potter* series and the foul thing into which the mayor transforms during the third-season finale of *Buffy the Vampire Slayer,* to name but a few. More common are tangential or metaphorical instances in which serpents are thrown into crucial supporting roles or used to show in an instant that a particular character just might be treacherous. A short list of cases in which snakes are portrayed negatively in this manner is as wide-reaching as it is astounding: a *CHiPs* episode in which an overturned van full of snakes antagonizes a thief; a scene in *Enter the Dragon* where Bruce Lee uses a cobra to scare the ninja pants off security guards; an encounter in the "I Can Read" children's book *Frog and Toad Together* that has a snake addressing the happy-go-lucky protagonists as "Hello, lunch"; the cheating lowlife who is chewed out by Paula Abdul in her 1989 number-one single "Cold Hearted"; not to mention a little book called Genesis. Even the smirky bad guys from *The Karate Kid* called themselves the Cobra Kai. "Get him a body bag!" indeed.

Nor were some heavy hitters of literature big fans of serpents, it seems, other than as a means to an end, whether by alluding to them as a technique to portray characters in a certain light or as a way to sound an ominous note. In *Macbeth,* for example, Shakespeare makes reference to snakes in a couple of passages, most notably to label suspected schemer Banquo a "grown snake," and also to have Lady Macbeth counsel her husband to "look like the innocent flower/but be the serpent under 't." Virgil in his *Eclogues* coins the expression "a snake lurks in the grass," a phrase that has become synonymous with a hidden danger or an untrustworthy person. And mousy, old Emily Dickinson may have been the biggest hater of them all. In her eight-line poem "Sweet is the swamp," she recalls an otherwise delightful childhood experience that was ruined by the appearance of a serpent:

> *Sweet is the swamp with its secrets,*
> *Until we meet a snake;*
> *'Tis then we sigh for houses,*
> *And our departure take*

At that enthralling gallup
That only childhood knows.
A snake is summer's treason,
And guile is where it goes.

Highest on the list of pop culture nuggets blaspheming the name of snakes, though, has to be *Raiders of the Lost Ark*. At issue is the character Indiana Jones himself, who is seemingly invincible in every way except one: He has an irrational fear of snakes. In much the same way that being a fan of plucky Rikki-Tikki-Tavi provoked in me an early distaste for serpents, witnessing a hero as pure-blooded and awesome as Indiana Jones being imperiled by something gives the audience the okay to feel that fear themselves, especially if the character in question is a paragon of masculinity and cunning. Given the long-lasting popularity of the film, the irrational snake fear promoted by *Raiders of the Lost Ark* has necessarily embedded itself in the collective consciousness more fully than that advanced by, say, *Anaconda* or *Snakes on a Plane* or the cheesy 1973 B-movie *Sssssss*. And this fear is not insignificant. Countless snakes have met their untimely demises at the hands (and boots and shotguns) of humans who were scared witless by them. It seems logical to conclude that this fear, irrational or otherwise, has been shaped, at least in part, by the manipulative way in which snakes are typically depicted in movies and on television. Exactly how many snakes have died due to *Raiders of the Lost Ark* is anyone's guess.

It certainly didn't help the herpetologist's cause that the film provided suggestible moviegoers with a tidy rallying cry when Indiana finds his aviator friend's pet snake in the cockpit in the movie's opening sequence, and yells, over the roar of propellers, "I hate snakes, Jock! I hate 'em!" That line had a profound effect on me, as it caused me to draw a direct comparison between my dad and Indiana Jones (and because it was abundantly entertaining to recite this quote to people who weren't named Jock). Next to Indy—that viceless, charming, wisecracking dynamo—my dad, like most fathers, doesn't stack up well. Then again, at the time the film came along, he paled next to even Sallah, Indiana's portly ally. In the summer of 1981, my dad was ramping up his involvement with snakes and alcohol, and by extension, his disinvolvement with my life. It occurs to me now that if I had been the type of kid who actively rebelled against his parents, I could have wielded that killer line like it was Indiana's bullwhip. Knowing that it would sting, I could have unleashed it at him whenever he dared bring a snake into the house or broach a subject as unpalatable to my nerd ears as the attractiveness of ribbon snakes.

But the fact was, I didn't hate snakes, and I didn't hate my dad. I was just supremely uninterested in the former and perpetually vexed by the latter. You might pin this detachment on timing—and it is the case that at age eleven, when snakes started creeping into my life more regularly, almost anything I'd come across that wasn't in my wheelhouse (TV, sports, video games, and computers, all of which, shamefully, are still in my wheelhouse at age forty) bored me to the point of yawning. More likely, though, my lack of interest in snakes was simply an inverse reaction to my dad's abundant fascination with them. After all, kids have been rejecting outright the things their parents are into since cavemen times, when Oog asked, "Care join me hunt mastodon?" and Uk said, "No, Dad, boring, me want stay in cave, play with new stick." I was no different, and it didn't matter which parent was involved. It's not like I was clamoring to listen to my mom read *The Canterbury Tales* in her fruity Middle English dialect either. So, because purposely incensing my dad ranked even lower on my list of preferred hobbies than listening to him talk about snakes, I refrained from unleashing that taboo (and, let's face it, sensational) line from *Raiders of the Lost Ark,* and our house was marginally more tranquil because of it.

Hilariously, after my dad took Mark and me to see the movie, he was delighted to point out that the critter Harrison Ford finds in the plane at the end of the opening sequence was, in fact, a docile black snake, and that the throng of hostile serpents that menace Indy and Mary when they're trapped in the sunken temple were mostly harmless king, rat, and milk snakes. "They're not even dangerous," he scoffed as we trudged across the parking lot outside the theater, as if George Lucas and Steven Spielberg had committed a blunder of the highest order.

All in all, snakes get as unfair a rap in the media as spiders and sharks, when in reality the vast majority of them are as innocent as dolphins. Yet, when it comes to dolphins in movies and on television, it's all fun and frolic, or Flipper to the rescue! Dolphins have even used their bulbous-headed wiles to convince us to purchase "dolphin-safe" products— and like everyone else, I'm more than happy to do so, because, come on, those guys are so obnoxiously cute. Maybe snakes just need a new agent.

Despite loving *Rikki-Tikki-Tavi* and *Raiders of the Lost Ark,* and even having a guilty appreciation for *Anaconda,* I've never been particularly frightened by snakes. Like you, I would prefer to have nothing to do with them, and I'd shriek like a little girl if I ever stumbled across a rattler or a cobra. But by foisting nature programs on me—lots and lots of nature programs*—my dad instilled in me at an early age a grudging acceptance of snakes, and in doing so, implanted in my brain what amounts to wary reverence of them. I remember a time my dad brought home a blue racer, roughly five feet long, as thick as a Red Bull can, and beautifully colored in a deep cerulean hue. Apart from his own selfish desire to have snakes around him, he'd bring the occasional capture into our house in the hopes that the love might pass on to his offspring. But in the same way he tried and failed to get us excited about Bob Dylan, Jimmy Carter, and grits,

---

* My dad loved nature shows so much that, in addition to predictably scheduled weekly viewings of *Mutual of Omaha's Wild Kingdom,* with inimitable, white-haired host Marlon Perkins, it was a given that he'd tune in if he randomly came across one while flipping around the dial—even if the episode was about something super-lame, like ponies. This became a major issue after we had cable installed in 1981, as it meant approximately thirty more chances that a nature show might be airing. While I usually enjoyed watching such programs if they focused on creatures like impressive leopards, hilarious otters, bodacious polar bears, or goofy orangutans, the randomness inherent in this flip-and-find method meant there was a real risk that you'd get episodes about gross spiders, dullsville fish, or prissy birds. To counteract this problem, Mark and I each acquired a sixth sense for recognizing nature shows a split second before our dad did. If we landed on one, we would zip the channel-changing lever of our primitive remote control quickly away before the outdoorsy images on the set sunk into his wine-besotted, forty-something noggin. But quite often we wouldn't be fast enough and he'd recognize the program, letting out a cry along the lines of "Ahhppp! Back! Back!" after we'd passed it by, and we'd be obliged to do the flip of shame.

we took a rain check on being interested in snakes, being far more concerned at the time with setting high scores in Asteroids or sorting through our sprawling baseball card collections. Still, this blue racer in particular was, for lack of a better description, neat. The tongue flicking out, the watching, beady eyes, the smooth, glossy skin—this is undeniably cool stuff to a kid with an inclination toward dragons and other scaly creatures from the pages of *The Fiend Folio*. And touching snakes wasn't nearly as gross as I'd feared. After my dad assured me that the specimen wasn't going to break free from his grasp and snap at my hand—a racer's fangs can break skin, and due to the prominent mix of bones, tendons, and muscles in the hand, it's among the more painful areas on which you can be bitten, although far down the list from eyeball and penis—I reached out and felt the snake's skin. I was surprised to find that snakeskin isn't the least bit slimy. It's actually smooth and dry, similar to the texture of banana peel or a garden hose. I didn't even purse my lips in disgust. Okay, I did just a little, but it was purely instinctual, like my initial reaction to oatmeal.

My relatively enlightened upbringing might, however, have produced an odd sort of disruption to what is possibly a completely natural fear. Recent academic studies, albeit much disputed, have argued that our fear of snakes—the scientific term for this is "ophidiophobia"—may actually be a routine genetic predisposition. Not long after the trip with my dad, researchers at the University of Virginia published a paper indicating that humans may, in fact, be born with an innate ability to recognize snakes. This conclusion followed up on a long-held theory in anthropological circles that the capability to spot venomous snakes may have played a major role in the evolution of primates. In effect, these theories suggest that ophidiophobia may be a good thing. My dad would never accept that assumption, of course, and even discussing this research with him resulted in indignation, but if you're a monkey hanging out in a perilous jungle, you'd sure as heck be thankful that your genes were encoded, essentially, with a message saying, "See snake, flee snake."

But luckily, humans aren't as bite-size as monkeys. Our comparatively broad shoulders prove to be a significant barrier to a snake's success at consuming us whole, and for this reason, only a handful of snakes in the world, such as the Asiatic reticulated python, the boa constrictor, and the dreaded anaconda, could even grow to the size required for them to be able to consume a person bigger than, say, Kerri Strug. This isn't counting the prehistoric snake whose fossil remains were recently unearthed deep in the jungles of Colombia. Dubbed the Titanoboa, it would have measured forty-five feet and weighed an estimated 2,500 pounds. Of this scaly behemoth, Jack Conrad, an anthropologist with the American Museum of Natural History, told the Associated Press, "This thing weighs more than a bison and is longer than a city bus. It could easily eat something the size of a cow. A human would just be toast immediately." (Hold the cinnamon, presumably.) Jonathan Block, a museum curator at the University of Florida, added immensely to the discussion when he said, "Truly enormous snakes really spark people's imaginations, but reality has exceeded the fantasies of Hollywood. The snake that tried to eat Jennifer Lopez in the movie *Anaconda* is not as big as the one we found."

Gigantic snakes like the Titanoboa no longer exist on Earth in part because average temperatures on the planet have cooled off significantly since prehistoric times. All species of snakes are ectothermic—meaning they regulate their temperature through their skin—and therefore larger ones are able to keep cooler in hot weather than their smaller brethren, due to an increased ability to disperse the warmth throughout their bodies. In the days of the Titanoboa, temperatures in their probable habitats were approximately five degrees higher on average—a scientifically significant amount—so snakes would have necessarily grown larger to compensate. Anacondas, currently the world's largest snakes, are native to areas close to the equator and top out at thirty feet now; most are closer to twenty, or less than half the estimated size of a Titanoboa. But scientists suggest that if temperatures do indeed keep rising as a result of global warming, bigger snakes could make a comeback—which could make life interesting for our great-great-great-great grandchildren.

While roughly six hundred species (approximately a fourth of all known snake species in existence in the world) are in some capacity venomous, only a fraction of them, including a few that are native to the United States, such as the copperhead, the coral snake, the cottonmouth, and various rattlers, have the power to kill healthy adult humans with their treacherous bites. What isn't reported on or publicized often enough is that the vast majority of snakes in the world range from being mildly perilous to entirely harmless.

Admittedly, this doesn't take into account the inadvertent damage that snakes have caused, like an incident that occurred in 2009 when Connecticut resident Angel Rolon flipped his SUV as he attempted to corral two pet baby snakes that had escaped from his pocket while he was driving. But you can't really blame the snakes in a situation like that, can you? After all, this was a man who put live snakes—plural!—into his pocket and got behind the wheel. (And yes, the accident would seem just as stupid if those had been *dead* snakes in Mr. Rolon's trousers.) Even my dad wouldn't have done something as obsessive as drive around with snakes in his pockets, unless maybe Bob Dylan commanded him to.

The snake in my dad's childhood memory, the copperhead, itself a pit viper capable of delivering a fatal bite to adult humans, let alone a stuttering four-year-old, is distinct from the relatively innocuous copperbelly water snake that was later to become the object of his conservational pursuits. The copperbelly, which laymen have been known to call a red-bellied black snake, is so-named for the striking band of red-orange markings on its underside, and, of course, because it is commonly found in or near bodies of water. These animals can grow to be up to six feet long, but most are about as long as your arm, unless you're Mr. Fantastic. Not even a human infant would be in danger of being eaten by a copperbelly. Copperbellies love to bathe and hunt in the warm shallows of ponds and streams, and their heads resemble those of turtles. I knew all too well what these buggers look like, because, beginning a month in advance of our trip, my dad had started sending me nearly daily e-mails containing close-up photographs of half-submerged copperbellies, with each missive containing the same one-line comment: "Our quarry is elusive." My typical reply: "So is my will to live!"

This "elusive" snake still lives in parts of Michigan, Ohio, Indiana, Illinois, and Kentucky, although it is listed as threatened or endangered in each of those states, which means that its future is anything but certain. In fact, as recently as 1982, copperbellies were thought to have been extirpated from Michigan, unseen there, at least in official documentation, since the 1960s. They were just one of the many species of unsung animals that slip through the cracks of bureaucracy or fail to muster enough scientific interest to effect change, and that would likely die out in the short term without increased conservation efforts.

The nearly forsaken copperbellies found some important new allies on a spring afternoon in 1982, when a simpatico friend of my dad's received a tip from a contact in northern Indiana that an orange-bellied snake had bitten a small girl. My dad was forty-one years old and had only recently completed his degree in natural resources management. He had no real notion of what his next step would be—perhaps get a job at the reptile house at the municipal zoo in Grand Rapids or find work as an educator at a not-for-profit nature center. Miraculously, the family who had reported the random attack hadn't killed the snake, nor had the police officers who had written up the incident. (According to my dad's unscientific survey, many snakes meet their ends at the hands of spooked or cruel land owners and law-enforcement officers.) My dad and his snake-geek friend soon set off for Indiana, just over the state line from Hillsdale County, to interview the little girl's family, who in turn told them that they'd already given the copperbelly to a collector from Fort Wayne. And with that news, off to Fort Wayne they went.

My dad told me that when he looked into the collector's cage, he audibly gasped. "It was an adult copperbelly," he said breathlessly as we approached Jackson. "I couldn't believe my eyes." But the random biting of the girl was enough to convince him and his friend that the region must be lousy with "coppers," as my dad affectionately refers to them. Eventually, they narrowed their search to a stretch of road across from a farm hilariously and impossibly owned by a man named Robert Zimmerman. There, after weeks of searching, my dad's friend nudged a pile of hay, and out one came. An obsession—and a hugely unprofitable career trajectory—was born.

That fall, back in northern Indiana, this time on his own, my dad was stalking the side of the road, Gandalf-like, with a potato hoe, when a car pulled up next to him. Posing a question that he would soon hear regularly, one of the teenage passengers asked, "Are you the, uh, snake guy?" (Word of outsiders, especially those sporting crazy hair and poking haystacks with anachronistic farming tools, gets around fast in these parts.) The boy disclosed that, while scouring the deep woods on Zimmerman's land for morels, he had come across a snake fitting the description of the one that had bitten the girl back in the spring. That lead turned up nothing new, specifically, but it validated my dad's optimism that these snakes were everywhere in the area. Later that same weekend, at a local diner on the right side of the Michigan border, he met a kindly old man eating with his wife who had personally encountered this very type of snake multiple times in the recent past. The man told him about a snake-infested lakefront property roughly ten minutes away from

Zimmerman's farm. The Hillsdale County address the man gave him was that of a house on Cellars Road.

If you believe in fate, this has to be it, doesn't it? What else but destiny could explain the circumstances that led Mark Ashley Sellers Jr., an obsessive fan of the music of a more famous Robert Zimmerman—that is, Bob Dylan—to discover a mess of copperbelly water snakes the very next spring in a swamp located just off Cellars Road? "To find a whole colony—babies, teenagers, mid-size adults, full-size," said my dad of that joyous afternoon discovery in May 1983, using a tone of voice that I reserve for describing how I met my wife, "it was a rare case of being in the right place at the right time."

As we finally reached Jackson and turned south onto Route 127, we were only an hour's drive from this very swamp.

THREE

The word "swamp" is likely to make you think of the sprawling morasses in Florida, Georgia, and Louisiana, or if you're a geek like me, the Dagobah System, where the *Star Wars* franchise's cuddly Yoda trained Luke Skywalker in Jedi techniques and—spoiler alert!—died. Such swamps, as we know from countless nature programs, horror movies, and episodes of *Scooby-Doo,* are teeming with bugs as big as Yugos and filled with gnarled trees that look like they're a lightning strike away from coming to life. Swamps like those harbor rampaging hogzillas behind every bush and conceal stealthy panthers. They're places in which you're equally as likely to be mauled by an alligator as carved up by a psychotic drifter.

The swamps of Michigan aren't nearly as foreboding as their more famous brethren in the southern United States (not to mention in a galaxy far, far away), and much of that has to do with climate and topography. Since the comparatively harsh winters of my home state typically freeze water over and compel many creatures—and, you'd hope, psychotic drifters—to hibernate, vegetative and animal life essentially starts anew each spring, thereby diminishing the leafy, pesty qualities associated with the more tenacious swamps of warmer climes. Also, there's enough drainage in Michigan to thwart a swamp the size of the Everglades, the Okefenokee, or the Atchafalaya; the ones here are intermittent and localized, a few hundred feet across at most, and that glacially formed disjointedness makes them more accessible and navigable than the interconnected, amorphous behemoths down south. Of course, apart from those in zoos, there are no alligators in Michigan, either, and that alone greatly ratchets down the threat factor. Unless my cursory research into the state's fauna was horribly wrong, there was zero chance of my returning to Brooklyn with a stump for a hand and a Captain Hook–like lament about a crocodilian nemesis.

The swamps in southern Hillsdale County belonged, at one time, to the Great Black Swamp, a geological bad boy that stretched for 120 miles from north to south and forty miles from east to west, largely in what is now northwestern Ohio and northeastern Indiana. Because the Great Black Swamp was thick enough to make westerly travel by land from the shores of Lake Erie arduous, especially after the thaw and heavy rains of spring, and in turn fostered malaria-bearing mosquitoes, which hindered settlement, the federal government drained the area during the latter half of the nineteenth century. This is why the bucolic Indiana and Ohio counties directly south and southwest from Hillsdale look nothing like they must have in the 1830s, when the

Great Black Swamp was so impassable that it even prevented large-scale bloodshed in a border dispute between Michigan and Ohio called the Toledo War. The militias for each side had such a hard time navigating the swamp that they never engaged in battle. Apart from the non-fatal stabbing of a Michigan sheriff by a miffed Ohioan named Two Stickney, the obscure conflict was a "war" of words, not buckshot. Somehow this seems like a warning to parents thinking of naming their offspring after a number.

There was a time when I secretly wished that every swamp within five hundred miles of Grand Rapids would be drained, or at least concealed by a Romulan cloaking device. While it was true that I had yet to set foot in a swamp myself at the time of the excursion with my dad, I had witnessed someone taking such a step—more times than I could count. Despite how hard I've tried to limit the outdoorsy aspects of my life to softball diamonds, beaches, and barbecues in the years since childhood, growing up the son of a snake guy necessarily meant having to go into the woods from time to time, often against my will. It was on these occasional half-day family trudges through forested back acres that my dad inflicted more swamp on me than I could reasonably handle—and unwittingly set me on a path toward being a proud indoorsman. If our strolls happened to take us by a marsh, my dad would typically vanish into the underbrush to get a closer look, leaving me and my similarly uninvested brothers to marvel at our fate on a mossy knoll. On rare, lucky occasions, he'd just stop and gaze at the swamp long- ingly, clearly wishing to investigate what might be lurking within, but ultimately giving in to some hidden pressure to get us home for dinner or a televised ball game. More often than not, though, swamps meant disappointment. In fact, the most frustrating moment of my relationship with my dad—indeed, the very incident that led me to realize with certainty that he and I were fundamentally different—took place a hundred yards from a small swamp. But strangely, it involved bowling.

One Saturday afternoon when I was twelve, my classmate Paul called to invite me on a family outing to roll heavy ceramic balls toward a set of pins, an activity that interested me about as much as watching tennis shoes tumble around in a dryer—which is to say, an unlikely amount. Paul was one of the few guys in my middle school with whom the prettiest girls in class actually seemed interested in talking for reasons other than soliciting help with story problems. It was probable, I figured, using the logic of a twelve-year-old dork, that he'd let me in on the secret behind this unfathomable trick, *but only if I'd go bowling with him and his family.* Whether to accept Paul's unexpected invitation or not immediately turned into the most important decision of my life, but I quickly surmised that there really wasn't much of a choice, as the two options seemed to be: 1) to bowl; or 2) to die alone. The catch? I would have to be at Paul's house within fifteen minutes, or he would have to leave without me. Paul lived five miles away, just far enough that riding my rickety Schwinn bicycle—even at top speed—wasn't a realistic option.

My mom was the preferred ride-giver. She liked to joke that her role in the household was Mom's Taxi Service because she was always carting one of us around somewhere, and, best of all, she flaunted her disregard for the speed limit and traffic laws as brazenly as the most deranged New York City cabdriver. Wherever she went, you might look out her blighted Ford Escort's rear window and see motorcycles, bikes, and other cars spinning off the road in her crazy wake. My dad was dead-on when he said that she sped around town "like a bat out of hell," and whenever he was condemned to be a passenger in her car he would lower his eyelids and offer up an exaggerated recitation of the Hail Mary.

And you really had no choice but to pray for your life when she was at the wheel. Just ask the man who, one dark November night in 1983, made the decision to jaywalk across the road at the foot of a small hill just as my mom drove over it—*kerplow!* Right into the windshield. As the guy's face pressed almost cartoonlike against the glass for a few uncomfortable seconds, a sight I distinctly witnessed from my usual protective crouch in the backseat of the Escort, it held an expression not only of "Owww!" and "What the. . . . !?" but also "This woman's a menace!" The pedestrian, who, it must be noted, had been drinking heavily at a nearby hotel bar and had stepped out into traffic without looking in both directions, eventually recovered completely, much to my mom's relief. But the accident forever tarnished her reputation as a driver you could entrust with your life. Still, she would bust every move, legal or not, to get you to your destination on time—and that's all that really matters to an adolescent in a hurry. Unfortunately, she was off running errands with my two brothers on this particular afternoon. I was forced to ask my dad for a ride.

It is a proven fact—I've conducted the tests myself—that my dad is the slowest, most deliberate mammal on the planet. Slugs, snails, three-toed sloths, and legendarily poky former Detroit Tigers outfielder Rusty Staub all look impatiently at their watches when they're around my dad, especially when he's asked to run an errand. Mark and I had learned that the only surefire technique for getting him into the car when it was his duty to drive us somewhere was to go out and physically sit in the vehicle, while sending Matt in every three minutes to point out in his cute runt voice where we were and what was at stake.* But with my brothers not around, I had to do my own pleading monkey dance after my dad agreed to drive me over to Paul's. In other words, I impressed upon him the *extreme need* to act quickly *just this once* by whining like a stinking little baby. Remarkably, we were on the road within five minutes. We were going to make it!

The route took us along a sparsely inhabited gravel road lined with dense stands of oak and ash trees that were incredibly creepy at night, and incredibly boring by day. To my surprise, my dad pulled over to the shoulder about a mile from my friend's house. He sat idly for a moment, and then turned off the engine. For reasons unclear, we had stopped along the thickest stretch of the roadside forest, through which you could barely glimpse a small, unimpressive swamp—so small that we may as well just call it Swamp Jr. I thought maybe

* Honking, on the other hand, would only make my dad go more slowly; it would annoy him further, and then he'd passive-aggressively have a go at schooling us about noise pollution by demonstrating that unnecessary beeping had a negative effect on him.

his Honda Civic might have been having mechanical trouble. But when I asked what the deal was, my dad rolled down his window, took a deep breath, and said, "Let's just enjoy the sounds of spring."

This kind of non sequitur issued forth from my dad's lips as often as the phrase "happy little trees" did from those of the whimsical and hirsute PBS television painter Bob Ross. After all, my dad has always found the destination secondary to the journey. Yet the words, whatever they turned out to be, never failed to stun. A familiar autoresponse, as when a wildebeest is felled by a pack of hyenas and appears perversely calm even as it's being eaten alive, came over me. I vaguely heard my dad saying something about how the tree frogs were just waking up after a long winter's nap, and it seemed like he was trying to coax me into reveling with him in their unholy chatter. Instead, I ignored him and just tried to focus on breathing. In. Out. In. Out. Whatthe. Helllll. Whatthe. Helllll. I thought, why in the hell couldn't he have made this pit stop alongside the swamp on his way back home, *after* I'd gotten out of the car? We sat there together, as silent as a couple of arch-enemies in sixth-grade detention hall, him smoking down two entire cigarettes, me trying hard not to cry. It took us thirty minutes to reach my friend's house. Paul and his family had set off for the bowling alley long before we got there.

When we finally did arrive at Paul's and I saw the "Dear John" note he'd taped to the door—which said, "Sellahs! You missed us!! See you at school, fool madool!" (*this* from a guy who held rich secrets about how to talk to girls?)—I felt like Clark Griswold arriving at Wally World, only to find that it's closed for repairs. It was difficult to understand how this could have happened, and after so much effort, too.

As my dad drove us back home, past Swamp Jr. and its hateful, chattering tree frogs, and I became convinced that the secret to getting girls to talk to me would never be mine, it hit me for the first time: How did I get born into this family? How is it possible that a well-adjusted teen who just wants to go bowling with a classmate who might throw him a social lifeline could ever have been sired by a father this willfully loony? Like a broken calculator or that dimwit in your math class, it did not compute.

All these years later, I have gained the perspective to guess at what my dad must have been trying to do that afternoon. In his own infuriatingly manipulative way, and at the perfectly inappropriate time, he was attempting to teach me a lesson. He was instructing me, in his parlance, to "reelaaaxxsssshhh"—to understand that maybe going on a bowling excursion with a friend wasn't as monumentally important as I was making it out to be. He must have foreseen it all then: that I'd bond with Paul that summer over Lou Whitaker, Bugs Bunny, and Spider-Man; that a few years later, during the height of the *Miami Vice* craze, Paul would invite me to join him on a family excursion down to southern Florida, and that during the long van ride down he would introduce me to bands that would become supremely important to the development of my musical tastes (and not only because the discovery happened as Paul and I took turns poring over a racy potboiler called *The Ninja*); that none of these events ever led Paul to cough up secrets about talking to girls, because it was entirely clear, by his admission of love for Dungeons & Dragons, the Atari 2600 home video game Yar's Revenge, and the collected works of J. R. R. Tolkien, that he knew as little about the opposite sex as I did, but that he had merely been better at faking it; that I would one day develop my own, occasionally successful method for getting through conversations with the opposite sex without feeling sick to my stomach with nervousness; and that I would finally, in my late thirties, meet someone who would not only put up with a furniture potato like me but also agree—and I have the legal documentation to prove it—to be my willing partner in crime. So, given that excellent outcome, even without the bowling excursion, why not relax? Or maybe he foresaw none of this. All I know is that he'd better have envisioned something profound, because it couldn't really have been about tree frogs, could it?

Although in retrospect I do acknowledge that, yes, it is important to take a deep breath every once in a while and to try not to take everything so seriously all the time, what I brought away from this incident when I was twelve was that disregarding social norms can cause you to miss critical opportunities in your life—that is, if you act unpredictably, you will not get to go bowling. In that way, the ordeal actually spurred me on to strive to become *more* normal, exactly the opposite of what my dad had seemingly intended me to take to heart. Not to mention that his failure to complete the mission—and make no mistake, this was an epic failure—also sincerely disappointed me. As the events that unfolded on this simple, five-mile cakewalk of a drive illustrate all too painfully, my dad had somewhere over the course of his life shed all interest in wanting to abide by the codes of others.

Being normal, in his mind, had become a negative; worse, he could no longer muster up the energy to abet anyone else's desire for normalcy. Even if that person was his own son.

I'm not saying that I don't have some quirks of my own. When you're a freelance writer who hasn't experienced an office environment on a regular basis for over a decade, you tend to pick up some interesting habits, such as wearing sweatpants to the bank, replying to work e-mails from bed after waking from your afternoon nap, and taking showers at five p.m. But many of mine occur mostly in context, and often to make myself laugh, like the chimpanzee noises I produce to confuse my wife or the beat-boxing that sometimes spontaneously happens when I'm stuck at an airport. I don't always live by the rules of others myself, either, and get called on it quite often. This is what you learn to expect when you have a chronic reluctance to do those hugs that everyone seems to want to perform every time they say hello and good-bye to each other, and when you have a questionable policy of discouraging offers to see photos of your friends' children. But I'm more Larry David than Mark Ashley Sellers Jr.—a guy who gripes about petty things and occasionally ruffles feathers, but who doesn't come across as the town weirdo or a homeless person. Except to my friends who have kids and like to hug.

In any case, you'd hardly pick me out as the most conventional guy in the room. Still—and forgive the two-bit philosophizing—I have learned, some of it after hard experiences, that there are things that a person needs to acknowledge as being important if he wants to get through life with some measure of self-respect. Most of these concepts, such as maintaining a reasonable level of income, health, and decorum, seem to have bypassed my dad entirely. Chief among them is the acceptance that being social and interacting with people, even total strangers, isn't a bad or cumbersome thing, and might actually be something to pursue enthusiastically, as long as you are doing so in a way that doesn't make you feel like you're being fake. For example, you will never catch me playing hacky sack, and I'm not going to square dance with you, but I am generally happy to attend your party, unless the bash involves Halloween costumes, cheering Yankees fans, or zero alcohol. Despite the volatility of other human beings and the very real potential that they will let you down, mixing it up with people can lead to ridiculous quests in moving vehicles, life-changing arguments over beers with friends, high-fives at sporting events and concerts, and rewarding work relationships. I even met my wife at a party, the kind thrown by an acquaintance for no particular reason—in other words, the sort that I had no obligation to attend. Had I been more strongly influenced by my dad's antisocial habits, I very well might not have gone. And if I hadn't gone, I would almost certainly be the same, slightly miserable person I had been before Megan entered the picture with her genius cat, George. Then again, had I adopted more of my dad's hermetic tendencies, I also might be living in a hut in the Ozarks. But you get the idea.

What happened in my dad's car that day speaks volumes not just about how he valued socialization, but about his attitude toward parental responsibility. Here he was, a highly educated father of three from a privileged background, having not drawn any income for the previous four years, living entirely off my mom's hard work ethic and his mother's intermittent largesse, and he was about to enter a line of work that, at best, might pull in ten thousand dollars a year. This was a sum that, even then, wouldn't have allowed him to sock any money away for a down payment on a house or for his sons' college tuitions, let alone instill our family's budget with enough breathing room to splurge on an annual vacation that didn't involve sleeping on a relative's pull-out couch or at a motel that advertised its nightly rate on a roadside billboard. But while other fathers traded in their bell-bottoms for cheap business suits and toiled in jobs that didn't ignite their passions in order to put food on the table, my dad refused to be a part of the rat race, no matter the consequences. Eventually, he became a man whose entire existence was an exercise in watching life go by. And here he was, ensuring his middle son's momentary unhappiness by stopping his car next to a swamp in order to let more life go by.

From a financial perspective, my dad's dropout mentality has been ironically limiting to the personal freedom he has sought to achieve. I've seen his struggles with avoiding creditors and keeping a roof over his head as a cautionary tale, but he has never seemed to learn from his own experiences. In dark times, most people accumulate balances on their credit cards or resort to selling prized possessions on eBay—I've been there. But I also know that not having come from endemic poverty, and having been lucky enough to receive a good education, I am more likely than most people to have the resources to overcome these kinds of problems, and that's something I've always been grateful for. In refusing to support his family, however, my dad was showing that he did not appreciate the educational and intellectual advantages he'd been born into. Since he had only known privilege growing up, perhaps his viewpoint was myopic. What he had failed to learn, or had refused to accept, is that ambition is not inherently a sin. Having a rewarding career, and the financial peace of mind that such a thing affords, is important, especially if you're partially responsible for raising children—his parents knew this, as did my mom, as do most people I know. Wanting to be in a position where you're not constantly worrying about money does not necessarily make you phony or evil; it makes you sensible, so long as it's done honestly. But for some reason, my dad had decided, essentially, to opt out of the American dream.

I must admit that it's a relief to know that, while my dad and I share certain attitudes toward responsibility and social mores, not to mention plenty of genetic code, I am in no danger of turning into him anytime soon. Proof of that can be found in the coincidence that I am now nearing the age that my dad had been when he'd stopped to take a listen to the tree frogs. It should be fairly obvious by now that I would never consider doing something like that.

My dad has never said as much, but it must be somewhat of a letdown that one of his sons—let alone all three, to varying degrees—has always felt so vehemently uninterested in spending time outdoors. Then again, it is his own damn fault. Long before the "sounds of spring" fiasco, he'd beaten out of me any hope that I'd ever take to nature. Not literally. My dad wasn't a bruiser. But he was a walker. Certainly, having an abusive father would have been a far more difficult burden, yet I can't help but point out that hikes do generally take longer than your average session of corporal punishment.

The walks/smackdowns were introduced into my life beginning in the spring of 1977, when I was a few months shy of turning seven. My parents had reunited after an eighteen-month separation that had been brought on by the many, many irreconcilable differences that should have prevented them from getting together in the first place. During their time apart my dad had relocated—"retreated" is probably the more accurate word—thirty miles outside of Grand Rapids to a rented, two-story brown clapboard house in the vicinity of the one-stoplight town of Saranac, an area that I later learned from teasing classmates back in the city was actually "in the boonies" or, worse, "way the hell out in BFE [aka Bum Fuck Egypt]." My dad had insisted that my mom move out to Saranac, and she had consented, even though it would mean an extra half hour's commute to the high school at which she taught and a farewell to the significant advantages of living in a bustling community—which for me included easy access to Big Gulps at 7-Eleven and chocolate sundaes at our favorite ice cream parlor. The only thing I remember about the day my mom, Mark, and I moved out to Saranac is that our friendly cat Euphrates bolted from the car instantly upon arrival and was never seen again. We should have viewed this as an omen.

Eventually our family came to refer to this dwelling simply as "the farm," because the property, somewhat preposterously, had a barn, a grain silo, and a chicken coop on it. It also sat on forty acres of woodlands—a vast curiosity, at first, to city slickers like us. Almost immediately, our dad led us on hikes up the steep hill behind our house. These hikes led to the woods. The woods led us to the creek. The creek led us to the field. The field led us to the hill. And the hill led us to the house. Three, four, even five hours of walking just to find ourselves right back where we started: a comfortable, temperature-controlled house where my baseball cards, Matchbox cars, and preferred television shows were all waiting for me (but not Euphrates!). Surveying the territories with my dad was marginally interesting the first few times we joined him, due to the newness of living in such a manner, but after a few months of exploring the same pathways, passing the same tree that looked like a troll, and hearing the same litany of *ooh*s and *ahh*s from my dad regarding the birds or reptiles we'd come across, this business of walking everywhere to get nowhere began to seem like an awful lot of drudgery for way too little reward. I failed—you might even say stubbornly refused—to see the point. But I never failed to let my dad know it. In fact, he still jokingly refers to me as "Iwanna Gohome" because of all the walks that were aborted by my whining.

Obviously, my dad's point in subjecting me to these walks—and to his credit, he was always happy when I came along for the hike, even though he knew it would only be a matter of time before I started moaning—was to encourage me to become acquainted with nature so that I might eventually fall headlong in love with it, just as he had. And this idea of rejoicing in God's green Earth wasn't limited to my household; environmentalism was growing in intensity as the 1980s grew near. Acting like responsible guardians of this planet by not improperly disposing of our Whatchamacallit wrappers was something every kid my age was being guilted into during the Carter era, most notably by the solemn, single tear shed by the noble Native American man in a recurring Keep America Beautiful public service announcement. The notion was being sold to me not only by my dad, but also through the plaintive warblings of John Denver, whose hit song "Take Me Home, Country Roads"—on heavy rotation on our living room turntable throughout the 1970s—even made West Virginia seem like a neat place to visit. The message coming from all over was loud, clear, and surprisingly similar to my dad's: Nature is good, people are bad.

When I looked at the environmental situation rationally, even back then, it was hard to disagree with that position—and this was before acid rain became a popularized symbol of rampant pollution (as well as a plot point of a memorable episode of *Diff'rent Strokes*), before the Exxon *Valdez* ran aground, before the "green" movement came into vogue. But I was also just a kid, and therefore supremely irrational. It became clear pretty quickly after moving to the farm that actively participating in taking care of the planet necessarily meant spending a lot of time outdoors—very little of which would involve games of skill. And so it fell in that category of things, like salads and calisthenics, that I knew I should get behind but was too put off by what I perceived to be negatives to do so with any real passion.

There were aspects of the hikes and living in Saranac that appealed to me, of course. Every guy has a little Grizzly Adams in him—this probably dated reference being to an impressively bearded TV character who, after being falsely accused of murder, flees into the mountains, befriends a bear and other wacky characters, and embraces his wild side. It's just that, unlike with my dad, who pulled a Grizzly Adams by moving to a house on a dirt road miles from civilization, my interest in being one with nature didn't go much further than what I saw on television. I knew, for example, even at the age of seven, that there was little chance I'd ever resemble the hirsute Mr. Adams (as played by the leonine Dan Haggerty), and not only because I suspected that I'd never experiment with facial hair. And I was right!

As we navigated through Jackson, my dad told me that his decisions to quit the ministry, agree to a separation from my mom, move to the country, and enroll at Michigan State University to study animals—all of which happened within a span of six years—had been spurred on by the very same thought: "I tried people. I wish them well. But I've had enough." As a Michigander now living in perpetually crowded New York City, this idea of wanting to flee to where everybody *doesn't* know your name isn't quite as ludicrous to me as it once seemed. There have been many times, especially during personal and professional rough patches, when I've thought about slinking out of town, under cover of night, like the Baltimore Colts moving to Indianapolis, and deleting all of the e-mail addresses, phone numbers, and addresses I've accumulated in my electronic Rolodex over the years. I'd just check out of the life I'd created for myself and start anew. Who would it possibly hurt?

Thankfully, those feelings are mostly behind me now that I'm happily married and no longer living in a slightly scary basement apartment—and it's not like I would ever feel strongly enough to act on such impulses as radically as my dad had. I have to wonder, though, if he truly was as content out in Saranac as he romanticizes. To be sure, he loved the solitude, the walks in the woods, the vegetables grown in his backyard garden, and the ability to brag that he lived on a property with a grain silo. But my dad also likes to mix it up with people every so often, despite his frequent bluster to the contrary. He likes to hold court—a main factor in his having been a regular at various bars in Grand Rapids in his thirties. Like most introverts, he has an innate need to break out of his shell now and then, i.e., to "prove it." And that wasn't happening out in Saranac. There were no worthy opponents out there to prove it to—no intellectual foils or confidants befitting a private school–educated, East Coast–born, former Lutheran minister with multiple college degrees, albeit a semi-functional alcoholic who would rather talk Dylanology than debate macroeconomics.

After nearly three years of this sideways lifestyle, my mom convinced my dad to move closer to the conveniences of Grand Rapids. It wasn't easy. But she offered a brilliant compromise: We would rent a yellow house on a hill in the suburbs that just so happened to sit on more than twenty wooded acres. Ominously owned by the highly conservative direct-selling corporation Amway, the three-bedroom, one-bathroom bungalow would offer my dad all of the benefits of secluded country living, only—praise Jesus!—it was right there in a prosperous suburb, minutes from my mom's job and within bike-riding distance to a Big Gulp–rich 7-Eleven. Everyone wins?

After I got done needling my dad for the umpteenth time

about the "sounds of spring" incident, he said that he realized while we were living out at the farm that I would never be a chip off the old block, nor would either of his two other sons. Could his consent to move us closer to the action, then, have been a rare act of selflessness? Just possibly. Still, while he often wistfully recalls his days at the farm, I think he was ultimately happier living in the yellow house on the hill, too.

No matter where we lived, and no matter for whose benefit he made decisions about our residence, though, my dad was no helicopter parent. What passes for normal parenting today would have been considered blatantly overprotective during my childhood—the era of the latchkey-kid epidemic. But my dad's lax parenting style was exceptional even for that lenient time. A good example of how disinterested he was in micromanaging our safety can be found in a memory dredged up by a comment my dad made as we exited the highway to stock up on provisions in Jackson. "You actually have been to Hillsdale County before, John," he said.

He claimed this had happened in 1983, a few years after we'd moved into the yellow house on the hill and just before he and my mom separated for good. But I was skeptical; wouldn't I have remembered having been dragged back out into the middle of nowhere? Yet my dad was adamant that this had occurred. He explained that while my mom and Matt had been visiting relatives in Bowling Green, he had needed to head to Hillsdale to meet an associate at the site where he'd discovered that first, bustling colony of copperbellies; he had had no other option but to bring Mark and me along for the ride. Because my dad had been aware of our disdain for his swamping—which had by then grown into something of a social embarrassment, as Mark and I had both entered a staid private junior high school—he had decided that his best course of action was to drop us off at a convenience store a few minutes away from the copperbelly site, because he had known that it had a video game of some kind. And in fact, this news did spark a memory: Mark and I did once spend an afternoon at a hole-in-the-wall store playing a coin-operated arcade game called Pleiades, and we hadn't been at all worried that a sexual predator or hopped-up hick might have waltzed in and made off with us without anyone noticing (except us, obviously). Even though the game was a rudimentary and repetitive space shooter that we had played continuously only because there had been nothing else to do for miles around, the experience now serves as a neat slogan for my attitude toward the outdoors in general: *I'd rather be playing Pleiades.*

In his own inattentive way, my dad had been letting his sons be who they were—he knew that we'd rather have played the video game than sit idly without electronic diversion while he talked snakes for a few hours. And thankfully, he hasn't changed this way of thinking much over the years. But then again, I haven't changed much, either. I didn't tell my dad this, but on our short drive from the airport, I had already said "I wanna go home" in my head twenty times.

FOUR

We're in copper country!"

This gleeful announcement from my dad, which was way too loud for the cozy confines of the Subaru, came a half hour after a stop in Jackson at the large Michigan-based shopping giant Meijer to load up on provisions. The chain, which operates so-called hypermarkets throughout Michigan and adjoining states, opened its first store, with the amazingly descriptive name Meijer Thrifty Acres, in Grand Rapids in 1962; it is acknowledged as having popularized the now-ubiquitous superstore concept, which Walmart later took to greater heights. Meijer—which people who are obviously not looking at the store's signage call "Meijer's," adding that possessive in the same irksome way that people say "Barnes and Noble's"—literally has everything you need. Chia pets? They've got them. Live lobsters? Racks of lamb? Organic vegetables? Freshly baked pies? Any number of five hundred different brands of chips? You've come to the right place. Bicycles with tassels? Leonard Cohen CDs? Bowling balls? Fishing rods? Discount shoes? Jokey T-shirts imprinted with a map of Michigan and the words HIGH FIVE, in reference to the state's resemblance to a mitten? This stuff is all here. Most Meijers have their own bakery, florist, pharmacy, and automotive department. You can have duplicates of your keys made while you shop for small rodents, flat-screen TVs, and guns. That Meijer has trademarked its core business as "One Stop Shopping" is an apt slogan for a chain originating in Grand Rapids, a city now regularly used as a test hub for new products. If any city is indistinct enough to stand in for the shopping habits of all of middle America, my hometown is it.

The sheer size of Meijer stores—the original location takes up 180,000 square feet, and they've only gotten larger—invites chaos, too. In high school, when there was nothing better to do (and there usually wasn't) on Friday or Saturday nights, two friends of mine would hop into shopping carts and two other cronies would push these makeshift vehicles down the aisles, all while each pair hurled individually wrapped rolls of toilet paper at the other as if they were two gunboats engaged in a water battle. (I, of course, played no part in such tomfoolery.) At the Meijer I shopped at in Ann Arbor as a perpetually hungry, cash-poor college student, I would begin by making a beeline to the bulk foods section to load into a plastic baggie a few scoops of fake Doritos (i.e., off-brand nachofied corn chips), which I would proceed to eat illegally while searching for the items I intended to purchase. A poor, health-conscious friend of mine would regularly shoplift fish.

The first item on my shopping list was beer. Not surprisingly, Meijer sells beer. In fact, they sell lots and lots of beer. Literally hundreds of choices, all at competitive prices. As expected, I opted for a twelve-pack of Molson Canadian bottles. Perhaps due to my home state's proximity to Canada, or at least because of the similarity in weather, I tend to drink brew from the Great White North when I'm in Michigan. I figured the long days of snake-chasing that were ahead of me would pass a lot more easily if I knew that a cold one (or five) awaited me back in the cabin. Plus, I swear I had read something—though come to think of it, it may have just been on the urban legend-debunking website Snopes.com—about beer being used as a snakebite remedy.

As my dad and I loaded our cart with food and beverages for our two-night stay in Hillsdale County, I privately thought about T-shirts. That's because, on the list of swamping gear that he had instructed me to bring, I had procured exactly none of it. Don't confuse this lack of groundwork with lack of interest in our mission; it's just that we Sellers men are not advance preparation artists. We wait until the last possible moment to do a particular chore—yet it always gets done. In addition to expensive things like top-grade waterproof boots and breathable pants, my dad had suggested that I would be wise to bring shirts of dark colors, so as to blend in while walking through the woods. So, while he was busy searching for boxed wine, I slinked off, not wanting to clue him in to my lack of preparedness for fear that he might read it the wrong way. I quickly located two unfashionable charcoal gray shirts at the almost criminal sales price of $1.99 each. Breathable pants, schmeathable pants—a pair of my old jeans would have to do. And even though his feet were a size smaller than mine, I had decided to wear my dad's backup boots, along with a pair of white athletic socks in which I ordinarily played softball. I wanted to be prepared, but I also didn't want to make an investment of several hundred dollars' worth of outdoor gear that I knew I'd never use again. I'd made that mistake a few years back, in advance of my first skiing trip since the 1980s. I'd figured that I'd love hitting the slopes so much that the high-end jacket, goggles, snow pants, and thermal socks the salesman had talked me into purchasing would more than pay for themselves down the road. These expensive items were now chuckling at me from somewhere deep in the recesses of my closet. Still, my non-concern for outfitting myself might have said something else about my attitude toward this endeavor: Namely, that I was a bit freaked out. I knew this because, in addition to avoiding thinking about the excursion very much before I arrived in Michigan, I had also tried hard to think about what lay in front of me as infrequently as possible now that I was actually there. With all of our purchases stowed safely in the Outback, though, I felt more confident that I'd get through this adventure. At the very least I'd have beer. And I wouldn't have to share any of it with my wine-addicted dad.

Shopping done, civilization was relegated for the next three days and two nights to our rearview mirror. We resumed our westerly course after turning off Route 127, and we were soon whizzing past farmhouses, barns, clotheslines, tractors, cows, cornfields, and ginormous rolls of hay. One building bore a sign that identified it as being HILLSDALE COUNTY MEATS. Multiple driveways were made entirely of gravel. Two porches had sleeping dogs on them. The county, flush with the headwaters of five separate rivers, was as bucolic as they come. Hillsdale was initially settled with the idea that it would be an agrarian community, and there's still plenty of evidence of that. But over the years, residents have found out that the soil isn't conducive to large-scale crop production—and the local economy has suffered for it. As many of the mom-and-pop farms have died off, the community has changed. Gone, largely, are the subsistence farmers, replaced gradually over the past quarter century by émigrés from the relatively more developed counties in northwestern Ohio, just across the border from Hillsdale, who have bought up the comparatively cheap land here in order to build their dream homes, in the manner of Californians moving to Oregon. To service these new residents, who, not being native, aren't as invested in preserving the naturalistic qualities of the area, trees have been felled at an alarming rate; the resulting development has polluted many of the creeks and ponds. With habitats increasingly being encroached upon, wildlife has had a much more difficult time finding its niche.

My dad often refers to these infidels from the south as "FOPs"—fucking Ohio people. When I pointed out that my mom was from Ohio, he shrugged it off and launched into a rant about how Ohioans love to till their lawns to a fault, something he likely associated with his landscaping-obsessed former father-in-law. "God forbid our lawns aren't perfectly manicured!" he yelled out the window.

Over the years, he has told me about ruckuses he has raised over housing, roadway, and landscaping projects that

have plagued the area. Some of his efforts have been successful in thwarting residents' seemingly collective desire to run
paved roads everywhere, even through protected habitats,
and, as already mentioned, he helped put the kibosh on a
vocal minority's plans to build a motocross course near important wetlands. But, joined by only a few key supporters
within the county itself, his twenty-five-year battle has been
arduous—and it's one that will almost certainly lose mo-
mentum eventually, like many localized conservation efforts
around the globe. My dad knows that he isn't getting any
younger, and he realizes that the suburbanization of Hillsdale County will continue long after he's gone. "It hasn't
been the same since the FOPs started moving in in 1987,"
sniffed my dad as we drove past one of these newer com-
munities, which was built around a man-made pond with a
gaudy fountain in its center. "Up until then, wildlife had the
run of the place."

As we finally turned down Cellars Road, which was
unpaved, we were in an even more remote area than where
we had lived outside Saranac. This was the *real* BFE. As
we slowly drove east along Cellars Road, we encountered
no other moving cars. There were no pedestrians out for
a constitutional. The houses appeared to be abandoned.
It was almost as if the place didn't exist. Of course, like
almost everything in modern times, the specific location
could be found via the satellite function on Google Maps,
but even in that application—which in more populous locations can be magnified to street-level view where you can
see all manner of folks, from a throng of angry scuba div-
ers to a loopy famous musician sitting in a bathtub in his

front lawn—the images of Cellars Road were merely far-off aerial shots.

In many ways, the very existence of that useful but Big Brotheresque mapping service had changed the idea of what's remote; it was yet another battle that my dad was losing. Even when you deliberately removed yourself from being in the middle of it all, as he had yet again with the log cabin replica thirty miles outside Grand Rapids that he had moved into, a satellite was watching you—and the proof was readily available online. It's one thing to view the rooftop of, say, my apartment building in Brooklyn, situated as it is in one of the most densely populated cities in one of the most densely populated corridors in the country. As a resident of Brooklyn, it's impossible to think of yourself as "living off the grid," and surveillance seems like nothing personal, given the very real likelihood that criminals and deviants live on your block; not to mention that, á la *Rear Window*, you might want to keep an eye on them, too. Using Google Earth to view locations in the middle of nowhere, though, seems more invasive somehow; these are places where people aren't living in the kind of densely populated areas that allow city folk to believe the camera is trained on someone else. Most people in those areas—except those living in newer developments, such as the one we passed on the way in—live a mile or more away from their nearest neighbors. A satellite view of a wooded area in someone's rural backyard is equivalent not to an aerial shot of my building's roof, but to an image of the inside of my living room. Speculating about who might be using Google Earth to scout out a place as seemingly inconsequential as Cellars Road would be pointless, but unlike someone else, who might have suspected ex-girlfriends, employers, or secret government agencies of spying, my dad's mind went to poachers. At least Google hadn't found a way to reveal the hiding places of the copperbellies themselves—yet. This was how my dad would like it to stay.

When contemplating how willingly to take part in the telling of this story, my dad had asked if I might follow some ground rules. "You have free rein!" he had written via e-mail. "But I do have a request. You can make fun of what I did for a living. You can make fun of me. But don't make fun of the snakes. The snakes weren't the problem—I was. Also, could you not reveal where it is? Can we not say Cellars Road? Or what about not Michigan? Couldn't this take place in Indiana?" I allowed him the first point. After all, the tongue-in-cheek first line of this book was going to be "I hate snakes," until I thought better of it. Snakes were indeed not the problem. I had nixed the second request, however. It would have been hard to tell the story properly without specifying the where. I also didn't want to mislead—or misinform—readers. "Free rein," he had conceded in reply, when I'd told him that mentioning Cellars Road and Hillsdale County and Michigan would all be necessary. "Do as you gotta!"

His fear wasn't without justification, though. Collectors are forever on the hunt for rare and colorful snakes. They use them for breeding or, more distastefully, sell them to interested parties on a thriving black market for exotic animals. The copperbelly, with its vibrantly colored underside, certainly holds some allure for these snakenappers. "It's a real problem," said my dad.

He wrote me twice following the trip to tell me of one of his favorite accomplishments as a herpetologist. In 1985, a teenage reptile enthusiast gained his confidence. Hardly expecting that the young man might have ill intentions, my dad willingly offered up crucial information about the many species of snakes he'd found on the twenty acres behind the yellow house on the hill. Over the next few months, however, it turned out that this kid was secretly scouring the fields and woods behind our old house with a pair of buddies; my dad soon stopped seeing blue racers and hognoses. Suspecting poaching but unable to get the police involved until he had hard evidence, my dad worked the front end of a sting operation with the help of a local TV reporter. A year later, the young man, who had been collecting species to sell to a French coworker, who in turn was illegally shipping them to Europe for a small fortune, had been arrested.

So to reveal the exact location of the farm where the snakes were was a bit of a risk, I realized—even though I don't expect this book to be heavily marketed to potential snake poachers. But as I would soon learn, knowing where the snakes are is only half the battle.

We rolled into a driveway blocked by a rusted metal gate, and my dad said, "Boom!" He got out of the Outback to lift the gate and swung it open with an ear-piercing creak that indicated the hinges had seen better days. He got back into the car and drove a short distance down the dirt driveway, which was lined with pine trees, before emerging into a clearing. To our left was a picturesque lake; to our right was a well-manicured lawn; and right in front of us was a tidy, wooden A-frame cabin. This, my dad explained, was where we'd be staying. Besides the possibility of confronting snakes, the aspect of this excursion that had given me the most anxiety leading up to my departure had been letting my dad take care of our accommodations. So I could hardly believe that the cabin actually looked habitable.

The last time I'd let my dad sort out where we'd be staying, in 2002, things had gotten off to a less auspicious start. Mark, he, and I had mutually agreed to attend my cousin's wedding in Vail, Colorado. When they picked me up outside the Denver airport, my dad leaned out of the rental car window and said, exuberantly, "Here he be!" He was wearing the howling-wolf sweatshirt.

My dad, ever the cheapskate, had asked if the three of us might share the same hotel room to cut down on costs. In hindsight, I should have insisted on paying for something that jibed better with my need for total sleep comfort. Being the older brother and therefore able to lay claim to marginally more satisfactory sleeping arrangements, Mark had called dibs on one of the two queen-size beds; my dad and I were consigned to the other mattress. In the morning, my dad got up early—too early for my taste, considering the handful of beers we'd consumed the evening before—and began fussing clumsily with the in-room coffeemaker. His fumbling was so loud that Mark leapt up and unceremoniously ripped the cord out of the socket, while barking, "No coffee for you!" Mark immediately returned to his bed, at which point, with the covers pulled up to my groggy eyeballs, I proceeded to laugh as if it was the funniest thing that had ever happened—because it was. My fellow travelers quickly joined in, and my dad's unfortunate room selection was all but forgiven.

But on the drive up the mountain west of Denver later that morning, I crabbed long and hard about the quality of the food at the dingy restaurant at which Mark had decided we'd eat breakfast. I also complained about how much my flight out had sucked, about how cold Denver was in September, about the fact that it was raining, about how I wasn't looking forward to seeing where we'd be sleeping in Vail, and about having to wear a suit at the wedding. My dad and brother tolerated all of this nobly. But when I bitched about Mark's fifth request to stop at a scenic overlook to take more photos of mountain vistas, Mark lost it.

"You have no redeeming qualities!" he fumed from behind the wheel of the rental car as we drove upwards. "You have no redeeming qualities whatsoever! No! Redeeming! Qualities!"

His outburst was severely harsh, but I also knew that I'd been complaining nonstop the entire day. There was nothing else to do but to sit there and take it. Sometimes when I gripe, I don't really mean what I say—it's just boredom, nervousness, or mild annoyance getting the better of me. Well into my adulthood, acting like a rational human being has been something that I have always had to work on when I'm around my family. In my day-to-day life in New York, I tend to curb any ingrained tendency toward nonstop complaining, because I'm aware that no one wants to hang around a guy with nothing positive to say. But for some reason, that self-awareness melts away once I'm around the people I grew up with. It's as if I revert to the annoying, not-fully-matured version of myself that I was at ten, when being the bother-some younger brother was the only role I knew. Despite what it must have sounded like, I was actually having quite a good time in Colorado. We'd played trivia the previous night at a brewpub that had delicious burgers. I was happy to be able to reconnect with Mark, with whom I shared a ton of history and a multitude of interests, yet whom I rarely got to spend time with, given that I had settled in New York and he'd landed in Chicago. And my dad was in rare form, purposely saying things like "the which?" in the name of fostering nostalgia. Nor did my litany of complaints actually indicate that I was unhappy in general. Other than the grim reality that having just spent a summer drinking and gorg-ing at barbecues would make fitting into my suit difficult, the state of my life was pretty much excellent. But by grip-ing about everything, I was constructing a little insurance policy for myself against disappointment. If I had already pointed out how flawed everything was—how doomed we all were—nothing could let me down. What I didn't factor in is how much my complaints could bother my brother, whose outlook as a type-A kind of guy has always been relentlessly optimistic. I was killing his good mood for no reason.

After his outburst, the car fell into an uneasy silence. After a few minutes of driving up the mountain while we all intently listened to the hum of the rental's fuel-injected V6 engine, Mark admitted that he had been a little extreme in his judgment of me. "Okay," he chided, "you do have *some* redeeming qualities. I guess." My dad let out a bellowing sigh of relief; seeing his sons at odds had been hard for him to sit through—he just wanted us all to have a good time.

His deliberate overreaction caused us all to laugh hard. Soon I was mocking my brother's lambasting of me, and things returned to normal. From that point forward, I outwardly showed that I was having fun, and I didn't even protest when Mark pulled over to take pictures of a rainbow.

The camaraderie ratcheted up even more once we stopped off in Leadville, a half hour away from Vail. Situated at 10,430 feet, Leadville, Colorado, claimed to be the highest incorporated town in the world. And who'd doubt that? While I fetched coffee for everyone at a nearby café, my dad and brother entered a faux trading post. When they emerged, my dad was holding a tiny paper bag in his stronger hand.

"Ooh," I asked, "what's in the bag?"

"Gifts," he said.

I made the international hand gesture for "let me look inside your bag." He opened it to reveal what looked like a plaster rendering of a shark's tooth. "Jawshhh," he said proudly. Slurring words was an affectation he'd recently picked up—one only slightly less ridiculous than Madonna's suddenly British accent, though at least he can chalk his up to a technique to combat his stutter. I did not ask him why my cousin, a well-off Texan now working for an energy company in Singapore, would have any interest in a fake shark's tooth bought in a town 10,430 feet above sea level. I did laugh, however. But that wasn't all the bag contained. Underneath the tooth lurked a fake gold nugget. I asked my dad how much he'd spent for the two gifts combined.

"Eight dollars," he said, then squinted, reconsidering. "Actually, seven ninety-five."

The next day, the three of us hit the wedding. I knew my dad was going to embarrass me sometime—but how, and when? It was going to be a game of humiliation roulette. At the church, we were greeted by my uncle, a well-mannered lawyer. My dad, obviously unknowledgeable about wedding customs, despite numerous opportunities to familiarize himself, brandished his offering. "Where shall I put it?" he asked. I will always remember the look of playful incredulity on my uncle's face as he looked down at the small brown bag my dad was holding and said, "Just hold on to it until the reception, Mark."

The reception took place on top of a mountain. During the ski-lift climb, my dad kept saying, "Gooah! Gooah!"; the three strangers huddled across from us tittered nervously. Up in the lodge, my dad dropped the paper sack on the gift table next to a large box adorned with a pink polka dot bow that screamed "saucepan." I carefully placed my neatly wrapped gift on the table and flagged down the nearest waiter, asking for a tray of alcohol. But at dinner, as we sat with grinning Texans and distant relatives, a surprising thing happened: nothing. When the waiter asked him if he wanted coffee, he didn't say something ridiculous, such as, "And the tar baby, he don't say nothin'."

From time to time I'd eye the paper bag among the other gifts. I'd think about my cousin and his wife opening their new tooth-and-nugget set and I'd wince. But as my dad chatted calmly near the dance floor with my aunt, looking—what's the word?—normal, I realized that maybe he was onto something. I mean, it's quite likely that his gift wouldn't soon be forgotten, and of course that means that neither would he. I, on the other hand, gave the newlyweds a set of steak knives. Or a blender. I honestly don't remember. I guarantee they don't either.

That night, in yet another dud of a room reserved by my dad, my brother once again commandeered his own sleeping area, this time on the pull-out couch in the suite's living room. And so once again I found myself sleeping within arm's length of my dad. His incessant, alcohol-induced snoring kept me awake all night. Even more unbearably, he received a call on his cell phone at 7:52 a.m. from his new girlfriend, Tina, a woman he'd met in an AOL chatroom. My dad began talking to her as if no one else was in the room. "Yea-yesh?" he asked in disgusting baby talk that I immediately decided I never wanted to hear again. A bit later he said, "Am I your boo-bear?"

I vowed never to sleep in the same room with him again.

It was just after three p.m. as we finished unloading the car. Only a few hours into our trip, I was hesitant to draw any conclusions, but so far it had gone nowhere nearly as bad as I'd expected.* Of course, the real experience was ahead of us. Still, that the trip was off to a better start than our Colorado excursion was heartening. The drive from the airport had reminded me that my relationship with my dad had never been the problem; it had been the circumstances surrounding us.

---

* When Megan had first heard about what I was planning to do with my dad, she chortled in derision. "But you hate the outdoors!" she laughed. "How in the hell did you get talked into that?" She'd certainly drawn a better hand than I had in that regard; the trips her dad had taken her on over the years typically involved military history, Irish castles, or sporting events.

It occurred to me that if he'd received a massive inheritance, or had made a fortune off a ridiculous invention like white-trash novelty teeth, or, yeah, had just toiled like a responsible parent (e.g., Megan's dad), things might have been different between us. To have been able to live and travel in somewhat greater comfort would have made his eccentricities seem like exactly that, rather than pathetic quirks that were holding us all back. Regardless, seeing the chalet-style cabin, with the nearby picturesque lake and surrounding trees, made me pretty psyched to be staying somewhere with my dad for what might possibly be the first time ever. Our digs looked like something out of Switzerland—or, even better, *The Swiss Family Robinson*. I could almost picture a team of monkey butlers waiting for us inside.

We slowly unpacked the car, my dad occasionally holding up a hoe or a boot or a net and describing its purpose vis-à-vis snake tracking. My fear, which was really just an ingrained reluctance to travel outside of my comfort zone, was dissipating. That's in no small part because I saw how much he was enjoying this. He was handing me items from his trunk as if each were a Christmas present. It helped that I was getting back that childhood mind-set, long banished by a cynicism brought on by one too many grade school teasings, one too many mouth-breathers getting ahead, and one too many years of living in cramped, smelly New York. Being alone with my dad, whose questionable demeanor and slow-poke ways had many times in my youth driven me over the brink of exasperation, was reminding me of one of the better aspects of having been a kid: You had the freedom to focus on just enjoying yourself. You could simply go with the flow, even if it wasn't completely for you. You could always blame someone else for your misery later. It was the beneficial flip-side of not being the master of your own destiny.

I was on my way to that childlike, carefree zone. But damn if those weren't hornets. Or wasps. Or some other species of stinging, flying thing. They were literally coming out of the eaves of the house, not to attack, per se—but they might as well have been. "I hope that's not a yellow jacket," I scribbled in my notebook, as one buzzed near me and landed on a backpack sitting on the ground beside the Outback. "Holy crap, that *is* a yellow jacket!"

I was kind of a wuss in my notebook.

And then I noticed: It was muggy as hell. It was getting to be late afternoon, and we hadn't even done anything, but the air was so thick and wet that I was already sweating a little. My dad, on the other hand, was veritably gushing perspiration. It was running down his temples, glistening his forearms, and dampening the eagle T-shirt in the shape of a large V over his breastbone. Such is the curse of the alcohol abuser: You sweat when you sit. You sweat when you eat. You sweat pretty much doing anything. The alcohol from the day before needs to get out somehow; some of it oozes out from your pores. My dad usually carried a handkerchief or cloth towel in his back pocket or a belt loop, and taking a break, he pulled out a grody-looking, ages-old rag to wipe his brow. "It's a hot one," he said, as though that would explain it all.

After we unloaded all of our gear, we checked out the interior of the sparsely appointed, though entirely livable house. My initial assumption that it would be a comfortable place to spend the night seemed correct. It had floor-to-ceiling picture windows, not to mention a workable toilet and shower. Most importantly, though, I discovered that I would get my own bed. In my own bedroom. With a door that shut. Things were looking up.

FIVE

I would have liked to wash up after my flight, but my dad started jabbering about "the heat of the day." This expression, coined and minted by Mark Ashley Sellers Jr. circa 1985, refers to a period of time on vibrant, sunny summer days, usually in the afternoon, when, according to him, not even devils can exist in Hades. In layman's terms, the heat of the day translates as "those uncomfortable hours when it's Borneo hot, even in the shade." My dad loathes this midday stretch as much as Khan hated Kirk; it should go without saying that he vastly prefers "the cool of the day," those happy moments following the heat of the day when the sun is in decline and the temperature is noticeably a few degrees lower.

These two terms have never made any sense to me either. All I know is that the sundial in my dad's brain had just inched into "cool of the day" territory, and this was why he looked visibly antsy to check out the shores of the lake. Not only was this section of the late afternoon more agreeable with my dad's comfort level, it was optimal for viewing copperbellies, as well. In the morning, snakes are hungry and in search of food. As the day moves on and the heat rises, they tend to sit on logs and rocks digesting their meals and warming themselves in the sun. And then they're after food again in the late afternoon and early evening—i.e., the cool of the day—much like a retiree in Boca Raton.

Copperbellies dine primarily on frogs, toads, tadpoles, and crayfish, and they consume these unfortunate creatures whole, in the way that some of us inhale pepperoni pizza. This macabre trick would be difficult for such a slender animal to perform were it not for its impressive power to unhinge its jaws. While I would have preferred looking for inactive snakes with hinged jaws, my dad pointed out that the best opportunity for us to see copperbellies moving around would be during their prime hunting hours.

As we set about to exit the chalet, I began to worry about the flies. And the mosquitoes. Starting in mid-May and running right through August, mosquitoes and biting flies perpetually buzz about, looking for blood. Your blood. It was a pretty nasty idea to think about—which I had been doing with regularity. Mosquitoes inject their saliva into you to displace the blood they seek. While this is a kind of natural marvel, it also means that, after a full day of walking around outdoors without repellant, or after it has worn off, you might very well have a thimble of mosquito saliva in your veins. Gruesome.

So, prior to the trip, I had made a bold declaration: Mosquitoes, my mortal enemy, would not get me! My basic strategy was to dress so that every inch of my skin below the neck was covered with clothing, and then to apply enough bug spray to kill a donkey. And so, despite it being a stagnant 85 degrees outside (this was the *cool* of the day?), and despite my dad's urgings for us to get a move on, I spent more than twenty minutes putting on the two $1.99 undershirts from Meijer, a long-sleeved shirt from home, a loaned pair of gardener's gloves, and old blue jeans. My dad—who had taken the eagle-emblazoned T-shirt off, exposing a pot-belly and a farmer's tan, and who was now clad only in khakis, gray sneakers, and tube socks—was already waiting for me in the living room after I'd properly armored myself against mosquitoes. I watched as he sprayed high-concentration DEET all over himself, including his head. Industrial-strength DEET is nasty stuff. When inhaled, it can lead to a chronic cough, insomnia, and even brain damage—which, come to think of it, might explain a thing or two about my dad. "I know it's bad," he said, "but it ain't killed or crippled me yet." He swore that DEET had proven to be a reliable weapon against biting insects, so I sprayed the stuff everywhere below my neck, closing my eyes and mouth as if underwater. Forget the war on drugs; this was the war on bugs.

And then we were off. As we exited the chalet, I felt like Frodo being flushed out of his hobbit hole and sent on a journey of great importance; this exhilaratingly geeky feeling was only heightened when my dad handed me a walking stick. "These are good for checking depths of waters," he said. As a budding nerd gorging on J.R.R. Tolkien in junior high, I identified most with Frodo, as I was similarly compelled by outside forces (my mom) to set off on a perilous mission (going to school every day) by unfortunate circumstance (I was twelve). But as I ran over our current objective in my mind, I realized that the mission hewed more closely to the adventures of Bilbo Baggins in *The Hobbit,* a more lighthearted story involving treasure and dragons; sadly, I couldn't compare today's trek to a quest to save all mankind. Our plan was less ambitious, as well: a quick survey of the two most approachable snake habitats closest to the cabin, and my first taste of swamping.

We trudged fifteen paces down to the edge of the lake and began walking slowly along its western edge. Oaks and hickories lined the shores elsewhere, but here, nearest to the cabin, a large swath of grass had been newly mown, and a small crescent of sand and gravel formed a poor man's beach. My dad guided us along this manicured section and probed the water intermittently with his stick to check under vegetation. Two short minutes into the easy stroll, I saw something moving in the water. A tiny head peeked out next to a small patch of algae—but it was so small that I was unsure what it might have been. A turtle? A lizard? Whatever it was, it was definitely reptilian. I pointed it out to my dad, and he yelled, "Boom! Good eyes!" He said that it was a baby snake, possibly a copperbelly but more likely a black snake. In his prime, he might have lunged into the water after the snake to confirm what species it was, but this time he merely wiped his sweaty brow with the sketchy rag and said, "Good one, suh."

And then, a minute later, I spotted another small snake nearby, this one flashing a bright orange color on its underbelly. This, my dad announced proudly, was my first copperbelly. Inappropriate cockiness ensued. Our quick success impelled me to think, Big whoop, these suckers are a dime a dozen, and I jokingly hissed, "Where are the big ones? You know, like in *Anaconda*." My dad laughed and told me about Big Mama, the biggest copperbelly he had ever seen, and it made me instantly rethink my smug position. I remembered him showing me a photo of her sometime in the 1980s; it depicted my dad standing knee-deep in this very lake, holding the kind of obscenely large water snake that, upon reflection, I would very much like to avoid encountering. He claimed that Big Mama measured six feet in length and was as thick as a baseball bat. More pertinently, he also insinuated that she could conceivably still have been lurking somewhere nearby.

Undisturbed, a copperbelly in a healthy population can live upwards of thirty years. The problem, of course, was the "undisturbed" part. While I nervously checked the weeds and grass around my feet, my dad conceded that the ensuing rampant development surrounding the cabin—since the mid-1980s, a substantial number of new houses had been built nearby and some formerly dirt-track roads had been paved—would have imperiled Big Mama on her migrations between the area's various swamps. She might also have been run over by a car while crossing from one roadside basin to another, he said, referring to snakes that have been killed by cars as DORs, short for "deceased on the road." And simple old age could have gotten her, as well. In any case, it was doubtful Big Mama was still around. I wasn't sure whether to be relieved or saddened by that. Instinctually, I was leaning toward the former, but maybe there's a snake heaven?

My dad and I continued our recon mission around the lake. Neither of us was content to have seen just two baby snakes in the same area in which my dad had once found Big Mama, but no further serpents were presenting themselves to us. "This place used to be teeming with copperbellies," sighed my dad. "Until the dog." He said that the man who had lived on this property when he had first come across it was a kindly, elderly retiree who had relocated from Ohio. On the man's late-1980s passing, the cottage had fallen into the hands of his son, who owned a farm in the area. As the recently mown lawn attested, the property was still being actively maintained; as the empty beer cans near a charred pile of wood indicated, it was also being used by teenagers for bonfire parties. While the son had graciously given us full access to the chalet and surrounding property, my dad remained angry about the man's pet Doberman. After inheriting the house, the son would bring over his dog and encourage him to, as my dad put it, "go nuts"—scrambling after any ducks, muskrats, or, yes, snakes that dared hang out by the lake. My dad would never cast blame on an animal, and so he didn't accuse the dog of having decimated the then-thriving population of copperbellies. But, he said, dogs can be controlled. "Some people have their dogs do their dirty work for them," he growled.

We had only walked a short distance and already this hike had reminded me why I had likely never fallen head over heels in love with the outdoors. I was being assailed full-on by deer flies. Every bug seemed like a missile—big, black, buzzing missiles coming at me from all sides. They weren't biting, but they were scoping me out, waiting for the moment when the DEET forcefield diminished in power. I imagined the scratching, the swelling, and the Cortaid that awaited me in the near future. I couldn't decide what was worse—that thought, or the smell of the DEET itself, which reminded me of hospitals.

Then there was my outfit: completely inappropriate for a day as hot as this. Why had I not followed my dad's salient advice and procured breathable pants in advance of the trip? Why was I wearing two T-shirts *plus* a long-sleeved shirt? Why hadn't I remedied the situation at Meijer? My dad had sent me extensive instructions about what to bring, after all, and I'd even glanced at them a few times. Yet somehow I'd failed to suck it up and procure the items that he'd told me to—ridiculous. I had imagined all along that this trip would somehow change me. But losing fifty pounds via sweating and a bout with heat exhaustion wasn't what I had been thinking of.

Maybe I was reading too much into my shocking, pathetic, contemptible lack of preparation, though. It was, of course, ingrained behavior. In fact, my innate aversion to prep work is one of the main reasons I don't camp. There's too much to read, too many things to buy in order to camp properly. Not that camping could ever really be my thing anyhow. The one time I attempted to camp as an adult, I made it through exactly one night in the wild. Fifteen years ago, three friends and I had planned to spend a long weekend in the Great Smoky Mountains National Park in Tennessee. At first, the idea had been thrilling—I was going to be sleeping outdoors! Under the stars! With good friends! But then reality had taken hold. While the other two guys we'd come with were seasoned veterans, and in general carried a greater tolerance for stepping outside their personal comfort zones, my tentmate, Phil, and I were novice campers. Not being familiar with the precise methodology behind responsibly shitting in the woods, he and I had greatly enjoyed a throwaway line in the park's brochure instructing hikers to carry a "small digging tool to bury your feces." But it also had reminded me that I was supposed to go number two in the woods, and so ultimately the joke had been on me. Who wants to do that, unless it was absolutely necessary, such as when your car breaks down in a remote area of the Pacific Northwest after you've judged a chili cook-off?

And who, other than Gene Simmons, would want to be roused from an unfitful sleep at three a.m. by loud, low huffing noises literally inches from one's face? When I had first heard these startling noises coming through the tent next to my right ear, my thought had been: *bear*. I had exchanged terrified glances with Phil, who had also been startled awake. Clearly, we had both totally convinced ourselves we were about to become some gigantic woodland creature's late-night snack. We would spend the next twenty minutes lying there, waiting to die. Making matters worse, we had discovered as this was happening that our tent was slowly sliding down the small incline we'd foolishly erected it on. The "bear" turned out to be just a deer—but deer can kill. Or at least maim. Or sass you. Or something. I mean, that was a scary goddamn deer! Phil and I would wake up the next morning twenty-five feet downhill from where we'd pitched our tent. Soon after, I had felt the urgent need to in-augurate my digging tool.

That afternoon, with rain soaking us on a hike, I had informed my pals of my great desire to sleep in a real bed in a hotel room with a real toilet. Another way to put this is I totally wimped out. Luckily, my friends had been easily swayed by my frequent mentions of burgers and nachos, so we all drove to the nearest town, checked into a ratty motel that seemed luxurious after the previous twenty-four hours, and went to see *Braveheart* at a podunk movie theater with-out feeling the smallest shred of guilt for having bailed on our original plan. I already felt like doing that on this trip. I contemplated suggesting to my dad that we call the whole thing off and go get pizza. Maybe *Snakes on a Plane 2: Fangs for Nothing* had secretly been released and was play-ing somewhere?

But I resolved to push on. If the trip had had any im-pact so far, it was that I was becoming genuinely interested in finding out if the copperbellies were still thriving. We'd spotted two snakes so far, albeit unimpressive ones, and while that had relieved my dad, there was still no evidence that they were persisting at previous levels. We obviously had more work to do, more terrain to survey, if we were going to get an accurate picture of the copperbelly popula-tion. Beyond that, though, was the rare case that I was into this gift of unmitigated "dad" time, a curse most of my life, to be sure. As we continued to circle the perimeter of the lake, checking logs and branches for snakes that might have been sunning themselves, and probing the shallows with our walking sticks, I brought up a subject that had always made me curious: the amount of money my dad's snaking pursuits had brought in over the years. I already knew that he'd made just four hundred dollars in 1983; not coincidentally, that was also the year he and my mom split up for good. He couldn't help but chuckle as I rode him about how little money that really was.

"I mean, now anyone can make more than that in a week selling sock monkeys on eBay," I said.

In 1985, he learned of a grant being offered by the federal government to survey a huge chunk of the Midwest—six states, covering a 400,000-square-mile radius—for an endangered snake called a Kirtland's. It was a massive job, two months of solid work, easily worth in the low-to-mid five figures to anyone else. He had to submit a bid to compete with other independent contractors, and wrote, regarding his fifty-six-hundred-dollar offer, "You can't beat this for the money!" They agreed. After revealing some of his other incredibly dismal annual totals, my dad said, "I never even thought about being a good provider. Never even thought of it."

And haven't I always known it. There used to be a framed portrait of our family, professionally photographed in 1978, hanging above our living room sofa. Splayed out on the ground on a pleasant autumn morning in front of trees with bright orange-and-red leaves, the five of us appear to be happy enough. My hand is resting on a stump; Mark peers out behind glasses with bottlecap lenses; Matt's a drooling lump of cuteness in the middle; and my mom and dad loom on either side of their three sons. But the story behind this picture is typical of my childhood. We initially couldn't afford to pay the photographer, and there was a threat of a lawsuit.

His lack of concern for our financial well-being has bothered me for a long time—during junior high and high school, sure, when I watched friends' parents finance trendy clothes, braces, new cars, and gourmet lunches, but also after my move to New York, when it was revealed to me that many people's rents (generally those correlating to killer apartments) were being covered by parental largesse. I was fine with paying my own way, but it would have been nice to feel like I could call on my dad for help if I ever found myself in a financial bind. Not being able to count on him in that way greatly factored into my not being close to him after I moved away. But it wasn't the only reason.

Until very recently, my dad and I rarely communicated with each other, except on birthdays and major holidays. The 1990s were not kind to Mark Ashley Sellers Jr. In fact, he'd admit to this himself; that era has to be the worst of his life. A few years after divorcing my mom, he married a brassy industrial-vacuum saleswoman; by 1992, their indulgences in alcohol and his itinerant ways had torn them apart. With no one else's income to draw from apart from handouts from his mother, and with little work other than the disturbingly small amounts of survey money that trickled in, my dad made the difficult decision to file for bankruptcy. He had already been forced to move out of the yellow house on the hill because he couldn't pay even the four hundred and twenty-five dollars per month rent. Though it couldn't have been comfortable for his six-foot-one-inch frame, he lived for a few weeks in his Honda Civic; later, he rented a tiny room above a store in Hillsdale County. Eventually, he headed to Washington, D.C., in part to take care of my increasingly dependent grandmother, but also because he really had nowhere else to go. By the end of 1993, a few months after I'd moved to New York, he'd hit rock bottom.

Back the following year in Grand Rapids, then fifty-three, my dad was unemployed and getting a bit too old to be spending all of his time in swamps for no payoff. He was thrown a potential lifeline when a *Grand Rapids Press* reporter contacted him hoping to follow him for a "day in the life of a herpetologist" fluff piece. The free publicity brought him to the attention of a construction company that was required to do due diligence on the environmental impact of a road-building job it had been working on; the foreman hoped to employ my dad's services as a consultant (at last, Lamborghinis!). The man asked what my dad's rate was. Without hesitating, my dad said, "Ten dollars per hour." He had been out of the realm of normal work for so long that he no longer had any idea what constituted a reasonable wage. Upon hearing this bit of news as we patrolled the far shores of the lake, I guffawed with disbelief—it seemed likely that he could have asked for sixty dollars an hour, or more. He went on to tell me, as we navigated through a thicket, "A colleague of mine later told me he was making seventy-five per hour for a similar job around that time."

More recently, my dad e-mailed with the information, the validity of which I can't ascertain, that just after he essentially retired from full-time survey work in 1995, surveyors appointed by the government began to draw decent livable wages—$75,000 per year and up. One university professor even claimed to have received contracts totaling a cool million for the same work my dad had been doing.

This, of course, had everything to do with the uptick in the economy, and with the money available for environmental and conservation projects under the Clinton administration. While I don't believe this entirely, it does stand to reason that the financial difficulties my family faced in the 1980s could have stemmed partially from bad timing. And of course, it figures that my dad, a die-hard Democrat, who shortly after our trip, would begin sending his entire e-mail contact list near-daily updates on the progress of the Obama campaign, would have been screwed by being at his most active during the dozen comparatively restrictive Reagan and Bush years.

The four hundred dollars he received per week from the construction company was nonetheless a windfall to him at that time. And it turned out to be the gift that kept on giving. After the consulting gig ended, the same company set him up with an office job, which he managed to hold down until 1998. That was the year his mother died and, finally receiving his (low-six-figure) inheritance, he bid adieu to the working world with some dignity. But he'd checked out long before that. Surveying snakes was his great passion, but it was a frustrating career for him, due to the many roadblocks and disappointments. He had slowly come to believe that the hassles involved with being a herpetologist who can effect change were insurmountable. Too many people, even those he had once considered to be allies, had let him down. And it didn't help matters that he drank entirely too much.

For most of the 1990s, talking with him on the telephone was trying, to say the least. No matter what time of day you'd call, he had usually been drinking. Eleven a.m., for example. Drinking exacerbated his stuttering problem and caused him to get stuck interminably on Ts and Ks and Fs; a phone conversation with him when he was in that state could try your patience. If you just wanted to call and have a two-minute conversation, it would inevitably last twenty. But discourse with my dad got worse when he adopted e-mail as his preferred way of communicating, around 1997. E-mail allowed him to lash out at anyone he viewed as an oppressor at any hour of the day, after any number of drinks, and without the stuttering problem. Sometimes I'd reply tersely or rudely to his long, often baiting notes; he seemed to be trying to stir up bad feelings about minor things—such as my lingering resentment about the time I got the flu at a card show and had to go home, only to learn on my sick bed that he had sold my prized 1964 Pete Rose baseball card for a mere fifteen dollars— and a pointless argument would snowball.

After one especially painful exchange, I let bitterness get the better of me and launched into a diatribe about the mortifying time the coach of a traveling baseball team I'd joined had asked my dad for a months-overdue equipment fee, and he hadn't even been able to produce a twenty-dollar bill. The next day, he sent an e-mail that said simply, "Why do we continue to do this dance?" And that blunt, frankly stupid rhetorical question led to a reconnection of sorts. I realized that fighting with him over past wrongs was counterproductive to our relationship, not to mention annoying. So we changed our tack. We began picking easy subjects to converse about, like sports and pop culture. Slowly, and often against my will, and without forgiving him entirely for the way he had treated us or especially my mom, I became his sometimes confidant; within a year he was telling me way, way too much about his new AOL lady friend. But I decided that too much information was better than the alternative.

I'd like to think we have a workable relationship now, one where I get to call him on what he put me through and he has to eat it. Instead of recrimination about how much he owes me due to the childhood he foisted on me, though, it's now something of a running joke. We see each other primarily on holidays but we're in touch regularly by e-mail. Our exchanges are limited to topics that are unlikely to stir up emotions, and thanks to favorable technology, it can happen on my terms, such as quickly hitting the delete key whenever he sends out a mass e-mail about something Bob Dylan–related. And, weirdly, this communicative arrangement, where I don't have to respond except when I'm interested in doing so, has solidified my bond with my dad more than any dynamic I've worked out so far. Indeed, at the time of our trip, our electronic interaction had all the makings of a perfect father-son relationship. So, why would I have gone and messed with it?

SIX

Finding nothing else of note while circling the lake—there goes my theory (and pants-soaking fear) about snakes growing on trees—we decided to decamp to the cabin to rest. Once we'd made it back inside, my dad draped a damp towel over his head to cool off and sat down on the lower mattress of the living-room bunk bed he'd be sleeping on. Disappointed with the number of copperbellies we'd spotted on our first short excursion, he said that he would like to go out again before it got dark, but it was obvious that he needed a breather. I must have been feeling much better than he had about what we'd already accomplished. Despite the menace of mosquitoes and biting flies, and the threat of heat coma, it hadn't been so terrible to walk around a serene lake, and we'd even seen a few snakes, too. Of course, I would have been much happier to have rested on such modest laurels than to have contemplated what lay ahead. That's because, later, we'd actually be going to the swamp where my dad had found his first colony of copperbellies, the one I'd failed to discuss with him for many years. I had few clues about what it might have even looked like. I was picturing a terrain that was impossible to navigate, in which huge, squawking, carnivorous birds swooped in from overhead and man-eating plants lined the non-path.

But a half hour later, we began a trek into the woods beyond the lake, and really, it was a fairly easy march up a forest service road and straight down a hill through dense, low-sprouted plants that, when kicked, emitted swarms of mosquitoes that thankfully disliked DEET even more than I did. The swamp at the bottom of the hill was tiny, maybe forty feet wide. The main chunk of that width was blocked from our initial vantage point by clusters of scrub brush—buttonbush, I would later learn—but we could make out the swamp water from where we were standing. If we were truly going to find out what had happened to the snake population in Hillsdale County, my dad suspected that the answer would lie within this small but all-important swamp. The site of his most memorable discovery as a herpetologist, the swamp held special meaning for him—and probably *only* him. To my dad, this excursion was a bit like two lovebirds revisiting the site of their first date. And I guess that made me the proverbial third wheel.

It had been a long time since I'd ventured this deep into the woods—not since the *Braveheart* incident fifteen years before, in fact. Now I was looking out on a swamp while standing shin-deep in mosquito-infested forest floor. It was an experience that could have been off-putting to anyone, but especially to a dude who, ten hours before this very moment, had been stuck in traffic on the Brooklyn-Queens Expressway. I've been living in New York City for nearly two decades now, and I don't believe I've ever experienced anything so dark, so silent, and so immersive in nature within the city limits as this swamp. I'm lucky to have lived for many years in close proximity to Prospect Park—one of the largest green spaces in the city—but I rarely go there for any reason other than to play softball or to take in an outdoor concert with friends. And anyway, it's always filled with other Brooklynites looking to escape their apartments. If you find any solitude, it doesn't last long. For this reason, many of my fellow city dwellers like to take vacations in remote locales. But I prefer to visit other cities and look for the bars, coffee shops, and bookstores I might hang out in if I ever moved there. And because I've spent all this time in the thick of civilization, even in my down time, the experience of being in the swampy nowhere was kind of a shock to my system. I didn't know if I was more intimidated by the natural surroundings here than I would have been before I moved to New York; I just knew that I was taking it in differently.

Walking around New York City can be a daunting experience, as well, in its own way. The smell of uncollected garbage and urine in the subway on a summer day is up there with any rotting animal carcass you might find in the wild. But I'll take those types of horrors, which I'm more than familiar with by now and which are always within easy reach of a twenty-four-hour bodega or subway station, over the unknown terrors of the wilderness any day. It was a scary place, these woods. Darkened as they were in the late afternoon by a thick canopy of trees, the woods could easily have provided hiding places for psychos with machetes. It was distressingly quiet. You almost expected something bad to happen. It's no wonder that the woods have become shorthand for "evil things happen here" in pop culture and literature. Everyone knows that Hansel and Gretel walked through the woods and chanced upon a gingerbread house where a hag plotted to eat them. But my mind was thinking more about *The Blair Witch Project* when I found stick clusters that I could have sworn were reminiscent of the bad omens in that outlandish movie. I'm not sure if evil things happened in the woods and people started writing about them, or if evil things started happening in the woods because people *had* written about them. All I know is that the woods have, and always will be, a place where crazy stuff goes down. And so I kept looking over my shoulder to see if there was an ax murderer on our tail, and looking up at the trees to see if an alien with dreadlocks and a laser gun had marked us as prey.

My dad had rid himself of primeval fear and seemed at home here. And so he wanted to perch. One of his preferred tactics for spotting snakes was to sit on a log at the edge of a swamp and scout the surface of the water through his binoculars (which he calls "binocs"). To get to the log, he walked through a six-inch-deep puddle of muck and navigated through dense undergrowth. After a minute, he reached it, at which point he sat down and lit up a cigarette, a prisoner to his addictions even in this pastoral setting. The sound of a striking match was something that I expected might spook the snakes, but my dad pointed out that the copperbellies don't have a sense of hearing—they react to vibrations, scent, and visuals. When he finished the smoke, he carefully stamped out the cigarette on his shoe and stowed the butt in his pocket; only he can prevent forest fires.

I saw where my dad had situated himself, but any desire to cross the muck and burst through the brambles to join him on the log hadn't kicked in yet. I was ready to spot some more snakes, but from my vantage point, I wasn't able to see beyond the cluster of trees that nearly obscured my dad and the open swamp beyond the buttonbush. I decided that I needed to get a better glimpse of my first real swamp on the trip without getting my shoes wet, reasoning—cowardly, perhaps—that it would be educational to watch him operate from a bird's-eye view, as if it were happening on TV. So I clambered back up the hill, and then down into an adjacent dell, and finally up a taller hill, over fallen branches and past nettles and around quasi-impassable tree copses. When I found a high place where I could get an overview of the scene—and from up there, under the dark canopy, the swamp looked more, well, swampy, with gnarled trees standing in the middle of the water above fallen, rotting logs and algae— I couldn't find my dad at first. He was no longer on the shore-side log where I'd left him five minutes previously. And then I saw him: He was on the move, using his walking stick as a probe and for support. Surprisingly, he was waist-deep in the water, wearing nothing but khakis and, I hoped, his tennis shoes. He was murmuring to himself, or maybe to the area of the shore which I had formerly occupied. From my new location I could barely make out what he was saying, but I did manage to catch a useful sentence: "The meskeets don't like it over the water." It appeared that he thought that I was still standing nearby, even though I had told him I'd be wandering off to get a better view. His attention had been so focused on the swamp that my departure must have scarcely registered.

"You're in the water!" I yelled. What else was there to say?

When he heard my voice, my dad swiveled around, seemingly somewhat startled to be seeing me in a different spot than where he'd last left me, but he kept right on talking anyway. As he waded farther through the water—which, with the sun directly shining on it, resembled a particularly weak Long Island iced tea—he gave me an unsolicited tutorial on his swamp dip. "Ya gotta watch out for the branches on the bottom," he warned. "That's what I use the stick for." I couldn't help but notice that he wasn't talking about snakes at all.

I made my way back down to get closer to him, finally reaching the swamp's shore. My dad lamented, still thigh-deep in the water, that even though he could recall a time when this small swamp had been teeming with snakes, he had yet to see a single one this time. "I just don't know where they are," he said. "It must be migratory. It's *got* to be." The disappointment—even sadness—was readily apparent in his voice but so was a glimmer of hope. But even though this special swamp had been a letdown, it was only the first day of our trip; there would be other, more taxing backwoods areas to search. Satisfied that his efforts would turn up nothing—which is to say, unsatisfied—my dad exited the water. He declared that he'd had enough and that it was time to sit and look at the lake. He wanted to cool off by drinking wine from a box. He'd certainly earned it.

His drinking had been more of the unmerited variety when I was younger. After we moved from the farm to the yellow house on the hill, my dad acquired a disturbing routine that bordered on an obsession. Almost every day, around three p.m., when it wasn't available in the house, he would ask my mom to drive to the store to pick up "the usual": a pack of Carlton 100s and a gallon jug of Carlo Rossi white wine. He would have bought these products himself, but my mom was, of course, the one with the pocketbook. From the time they got back together in 1977, until their 1984 divorce, with my dad slowly grinding his way through an additional college degree and deliberately shirking all responsibility, my mom was the sole earner in the family—not counting the small chunks of money my dad periodically asked for, and usually received, from my grandmother. My mom taught English full-time at a high school, but three nights a week, in both the fall and winter, she also taught classes at a local community college. After my parents divorced, she tacked on another part-time teaching gig and often accepted offers to grade Advanced Placement exams. Her demanding work schedule paid our rent, kept the lights on (most of the time), and put Ho Hos in the cupboard, but it also meant that my mom was consistently exhausted. Because she didn't have a lot of time to keep house and because the four guys in her life were indolent and childish, and also because there was no record of discipline ever being instilled or enforced by either parent, the yellow house on the hill was in a perpetual state of disarray. Dirty socks and shirts, stripped off while watching TV or playing video games, remained on the living room floor until she found the time and energy to whiz around and collect it all on laundry day. Bowls containing small pools of cereal milk rested on tables for days; even our two cats were too lazy to drink from them. Piles of newspapers, some almost a year old, were strewn everywhere. It was a disaster zone, plain and simple, as bad as anything you'd see on *Hoarders*. You were always stepping on something questionable or valuable—a forgotten apple core here, a prized toy there. This never happened at the houses of my friends. While other homes were much more likely to contain the pungent aromas of home-cooked vegetables than ours was, my friends' houses also offered chances to sleep in well-made beds in rooms where all the toys and clothes were neatly put away. Even if younger siblings were scampering around, the houses of my friends were nowhere nearly as chaotic as mine, and as such, were a means of escape. On the rare occasion that I'd allow a friend to come over to my place, I would worry that he'd point out and ridicule me for a discarded piece of food or an undiscovered colony of ants—stuff that I had somehow learned to tolerate, and even ignore.

The one visit paid to us at that house by my dad's mom, who had a team of household employees to assist her back in D.C., was humiliating. She forced Mark and me to take care of chores that our parents never even suggested that we do, and as we worked, with her disdain for the messiness dripping from her voice, she kept saying, "Do you want to be poor white trash? Do you want to be poor white trash?" But we *weren't* poor white trash. We were a highly literate yet lower-middle-class family with no interest in cleaning up after ourselves.

One afternoon, after a pile of books collapsed and spilled a bottle of Mountain Dew all over the Monopoly game we'd abandoned mid-match more than a week before, and we sat around marveling at the liquid carnage, Mark and I spent a few moments fantasizing about being able to afford a maid of our own, like on *The Brady Bunch* or *The Jeffersons*; such flights of fancy were common in our house. There was always a get-rich-quick scheme going on. My mom—rather than simply using the time to vacuum, or to teach her kids how to vacuum—dutifully entered all manner of mail-in contests advertised by outfits such as Publishers Clearing House. All we ever won was a basketball and an ice cooler. My dad tilled a small garden that seemingly produced nothing but gourd vegetables, and one summer decided the fruits of his labor would help pay the rent. So he planted a wooden sign along the busy road in front of our house that my mom, in definite approval of adding any kind of income, had painted with the words SQUASH FOR SALE. When Mark and I decided to sell some of our baseball cards, the sign was altered to read SQUASH FOR SALE + BASEBALL CARDS. Only the + BASEBALL CARDS part was written in the handwriting of an eleven-year-old.

Sadly, we were sitting ducks. Our family was dangerously, even humorously gullible, probably because we didn't have a united front. My parents had a combined seven college degrees between them, but what they did not have were street smarts. Or if they held any measure of accumulated practical wisdom, they were not very good or especially interested in imparting it to their children. While my father-in-law, for instance, sent each of his kids off to college with a homily about protecting their credit ratings and staying safe from would-be muggers, my parents sent me off to school with no special advice other than to call home once in a while. Throughout my childhood, each of us kids, essentially, was left to fend for himself. Boys from around the area, interested not in homemade squash but in baseball cards, would occasionally stop by. Two in particular told me years later that they would flip through our binders and feign great interest in our collections, and would attempt to get Mark and me to leave the porch by asking to see some other sets or cards that we hadn't brought out. Once we'd gone back inside to dig through piles to find what they'd said they were looking for, they would pocket cards out on the porch. Our parents, who were often inside, not at all worried that strangers might be taking advantage of their sons, were every bit as oblivious to the thefts as we were.

But anyone could have predicted that such things were bound to happen to us. We were five individuals without any knowledge about the rules of life. And more than any other, the rule we least understood was that there was strength in numbers. It was in the yellow house on the hill that my dad began to retreat from the family and we began to retreat from him. My dad isolated himself from us with Bob Dylan and alcohol, and, taking our cues from him, his sons followed suit (choosing more age-appropriate habits, of course). The arrival of cable television provided us with a novel escape mechanism. We studied MTV so religiously that at a certain point each of us could name the artist and title of every video shown on the channel within a second of the opening frame. Video games became a source of endless hours of blissful entertainment. While I loved hitting the arcade, playing Intellivision (the Betamax to Atari's VHS) was, crucially, something I could do at home. Being able to immerse myself in the frivolous worlds of music television and video games—not to mention fantasy novels and baseball statistics—made the yellow house on the hill bearable, maybe for the first time. Finally, I could just pretend I wasn't there, even though I was required by law to be.

And I did need an escape from the reality of our home. The house was small, charmless, and in disrepair. It had three bedrooms, lined up in a row on one side of a long hallway. My dad had the master bedroom, mostly to himself. Mark and I attempted to peaceably coexist in the middle room. My mother slept in the room at the end of the hall, with Matt. The house had only one bathroom, which would have been acceptable if it had had a shower. Four long years of baths. I will never take another bath in my life. Bathing in your own filth is not a good way to get clean, no matter what the Calgon soap people might try to tell you. We all lived this way until a series of fights between my parents culminated in a knock-down, drag-out conflict that ended when my dad threw a chair across the room and called my mom a "goddamn ice queen."

After we moved out, my dad finally got the solitude he had long been craving. Each of us instantly became happier. My parents' divorce was a no-brainer for them, but it was even more helpful for my brothers and me. Matt and I still got to see our dad every morning when our mom would drop us off at the yellow house on the hill to catch the bus (Mark had transferred to a different school district), and he stayed involved in our lives by showing up at track meets and Little League games, but we quickly learned the benefits of not actually living with him. My mom detested cigarettes, so our new apartment was devoid of the tobacco stench, and smoke no longer permeated the air and attached itself to our clothes. What's more, we were no longer forced to listen to Bob Dylan or watch PBS nature shows. Sure, it would grow tense when my parents had to be in each other's presence, or when one of them was mentioned to the other. But those things were a small price to pay for freedom.

My dad and I walked slowly up the hill away from the swamp. It took us about fifteen minutes to reach the house. We were hungry and exhausted, and while my dad rested on the porch and looked out on the lake, I went inside to wash my hands repeatedly and fix us a couple of sandwiches. I was relieved to be inside after a long stretch of feeling completely exposed to the elements. My dad, on the other hand, relaxed by staying outside, even though, as the sun began to set over the lake, it was showtime for the local mosquito population.

After I delivered a sandwich to him, he wanted nothing more than to eat, drink, and reminisce. His memories of our family's past tended to be more nostalgic than mine, but they were also tinged with more humor. I'd grant him this favor tonight; maybe another dose of his outlook on things would help me to look back on my childhood less cynically. So I decided to join him, but only on the condition that I got to sit on one side of the screen door—the side away from the bugs—while he sat on the other. That way we'd get to spend time together *and* remain in our preferred comfort zones. If we had been able to figure out compromises like this one a long time ago, maybe our relationship wouldn't have been as challenging.

Back when my dad was living alone in the yellow house, Matt and I developed comfortable rituals for our morning visits with him. After my mom dropped us off around seven-thirty in the morning, we'd all watch *Inspector Gadget* and play a card game in the hour or so before the bus arrived to take us to school. In this concentrated period of time, Matt and I got the kind of undivided attention from my dad that had been more difficult to come by even when we spent entire days with him. But one fall morning, when my mom dropped Matt and me off at my dad's, we noticed a rust-colored Nova we'd never seen before parked in the driveway. And when we entered the house, we noticed three people we'd never seen before parked in front of the television. More specifically, there was an entire family—a heavy-set couple and their pre-teen son—that we'd never seen before, sitting in the living room of my dad's house watching *The Great Space Coaster*. I was shocked not only because there were three total strangers in my dad's living room, but also because puppet news-caster Gary Gnu ("No Gnus is good Gnus!") was not a good way to start the day. My dad, who had already left for his new part-time job as a welfare counselor, had failed to tell us or our mom about this bizarre development. He would later explain to us that this was the Garces family, Central American immigrants my dad had invited to stay at his house, in part for the rent income but also out of a misguided sense of pity. To afford the rent that my mom's paycheck had covered before she moved out, he'd taken the new gig, and Mr. Garces, an itinerant construction worker with a wife and young son, had come to him for employment guidance. When this exchange hadn't amounted to anything, my dad had offered to let the family crash at his place, until better prospects came along.

We soon got used to their presence, but we didn't like it. One morning, Mr. Garces inquired about the Christian Reform private school I went to. It was run by Grand Rapids's dominant religious group—an affiliation to which my Lutheran parents had never belonged or shown any particular affinity for. Even so, and despite our limited budget, I'd been sent there starting with sixth grade for the supposedly top-notch academics (a claim I would dispute). The indoctrination into an unfamiliar and unwanted religion had been starting to get to me—so when Mr. Garces said, "How is that parochial school, John?" the comment became one more reason for me to resent him and his family. My school *wasn't* a parochial school; if it had been filled with wisecracking nuns and pretty girls in plaid uniforms then I might not have hated it as much as I did. Instead, it was a place run by religious fanatics who got off on punishing you just because they could. Mr. Garces's reference to "parochial" particularly galled me that morning, because while my classmates had been sent to the school for religious reasons, I had not. Also, my parents seemed to be perpetually and uniquely behind on tuition payments, and that set me apart from everyone else. My dad's leaving the Lutheran ministry when I was a toddler had left me with the impression that religion was nothing of consequence. So even though my mom had continued to attend church and encouraged us to go through the motions, I had had a hard time understanding why everyone at school seemed to get so worked up about it. Once, I had raised my hand to ask how dinosaurs factored into the equation when a teacher attempted to instruct us that the Genesis story of creation was scientific fact, but once I realized that my peers were staring at me in disbelief, I gave up trying to show him the error in his lesson plan. Instead, I focused my attention on surviving at the school, and did so in three ways: 1) by avoiding being teased about the way I looked, smelled, or dressed, even though I sometimes wore parachute pants, only bathed a few times a week (even after we moved to the apartment complex, and I had the benefit of showers, old habits of avoiding washing up died hard), and chose to wear my hair in the manner of goony Detroit Pistons forward Kelly Tripucka—a shaggy mass resembling muskrat fur; 2) by attempting to talk to Carolyn, who had a sly way about her and looked just plain enough to escape the attention of my alpha-male peers at school, because I wanted her, even though I really didn't know what this meant; and 3) by writing stories with my friend Rob, about two wacky crime fighters modeled after ourselves, whom he and I named Dr. Weird and Dr. Strange, respectively (I even wrote Carolyn into the stories as Dr. Strange's assistant, which I now see wasn't the best way to get her to like me).

The six months the Garceses lived in the yellow house—essentially my entire ninth-grade year, which turned out to be my last at the Christian Reform school—further strained my already tenuous relationship with my dad. The inexplicable presence of unrelated people in my dad's house was just embarrassing to me, as I'm sure it would have been for most kids my age. I had even made up a story about the rusted Chevy Nova in the driveway, claiming it was a sixteenth birthday present from my dad to my brother Mark (what a gift!). Worse, though, was that after they moved in, Matt and I had lost our daily dose of unadulterated Dad time, a fact he himself regretted. Six months into the ordeal, my dad bucked up the courage to ask the Garceses to move out, which they did without incident. But he later admitted that they'd never paid him any rent, and that the additional hits to his utility and food bills had actually put him a few thousand dollars *farther* into the hole.

After they moved out, I was thankful to have the house—and my dad—back. But the following summer, in 1986, a bossy vacuum saleswoman moved in, and my relationship with my dad virtually disintegrated. By then I was nearly sixteen, and had started attending a public high school that didn't require catching a bus from my dad's house or listening to pointless lectures from teachers about turning the other cheek. I was annoyed that my dad had taken up with a new woman so soon after the Garceses had left. In retrospect, I'm not sure it really mattered. I had reached the age when hanging out with my parents no longer held much appeal, anyway, no matter how comfortable—or devoid of TV-hogging strangers—their homes were. In some ways, my dad's inconsiderate behavior was just amplifying the normal process of a teenager growing apart from his family.

SEVEN

After dusk, my dad was still sitting on the porch, sipping cheap red wine from a plastic Dixie cup. I was next to him, on the other side of the screen door, quite happy to be in the comparatively bug-free chalet and pounding a Molson Canadian. We were talking to each other through the screen as if it were a confessional.

My dad's shirt remained off, and he had draped it over his pasty white shoulders to absorb any lingering sweat. He had on a pair of cutoff shorts that should probably have been a size or two larger. He'd also smoked more cigarettes that evening than would have been acceptable in polite company since the mid-1980s and possibly because of the influence of nicotine, he was rocking back and forth, as if jamming out to a song in his head. If anyone would have stumbled across him, there was a good chance they'd think he might be a schizophrenic off his meds. My dad would be entirely unfazed by such an assessment as he completely lacks self-consciousness. Well, he realizes that other people might see him as being strange, but he embraces this perception, in part because it jibes with the self-image he has of himself as being a rebel, operating without regard for societal norms. This has made him, quite often, an infuriating parent, at least to someone like me. Unlike my dad, I have always been overly concerned about what others think of me. Some of this probably has to do with his erratic and irresponsible behavior during my childhood; too many times it resulted in worry that a friend would drop by unannounced and see my dad five or six drinks in. But lately, I've come to understand that caring too much about what others think is its own problem, one that has certainly gotten me into trouble over the years—while I've found that the adage "nice guys finish last" isn't true, I can tell you that they certainly don't finish first. Plus, when you constantly modulate your demeanor to accommodate a given situation, you can lose track of who you really are. This is not something that my dad has ever been concerned about.

But however he was dressed, and whatever a random passerby might have thought, my dad can be good company in private. As he has grown older, nostalgia has threatened to overcome him. He loves discussing what he sees as being the great moments of his life, and sometimes, if events overlap, of his kids' lives, too. The bully who tormented him in grade school. The housecats we have owned. The ill-fated canoe excursion. These were all subjects our entire family knew by heart. But because he's so into it, talking about the past with him is usually entertaining, even though you've heard it all—or in many instances, lived it all—before. Such was the case with one of his favorite stories: the trip to Iowa. And maybe because it also involved a road trip, my dad brought the memory up through the screen door with a grin: "Remember Ottumwa?"

Hoo-boy—did I ever. There's a certain point in your life when you come to the crippling realization that your greatest days are in the rearview mirror, and objects aren't closer than they appear. Your desire to succeed is no longer exceeding your desire to sit on the couch and watch HGTV. If you're lucky, you will be old and withered when this moment creeps up on you and massacres your will to live, and you will have plenty to reflect on as you rock back and forth in an uncomfortable wooden chair, or however it is the elderly sit back and reflect. Most men incur this damage sometime in their forties or early fifties and misguidedly try to fix the problem during what is known as a midlife crisis, a time defined, in Hollywood terms, by too-young girlfriends, fast cars, and incredibly bogus hairpieces. Unfortunately, this happened to me when I was twelve, on the day that I learned I wasn't the best Donkey Kong player in the world. And it all went down in Ottumwa.

Back then, if the small Iowa town was known at all, it was for being used as the hometown of Radar O'Reilly on TV's *M*A*S*H*. But to Mark and me, and a small group of geeks around the globe, it was also known as being a kind of Mecca, only without all the burkas. Mustachioed resident Walter Day, who has since been immortalized in the 2007 video game documentary *The King of Kong*, had opened an arcade there called Twin Galaxies, but more significantly, had also started up what he referred to as "the national scoreboard," a self-proclaimed official reckoning of all the high scores for every title in existence. To get your score verified, you could call a phone number published in the back of a prominent video game magazine and talk to Day himself about your performance, which he would give a thumbs up or down to, like a Roman emperor. A favorable decision could very well be published in a national magazine within a few months, which, in the early 1980s, seemed like a lightning-fast track to fame—although from today's perspective, we may as well have been reporting our scores in cuneiform. Day, a P. T. Barnum for Reagan-era nerds, had announced that he was putting together the world's first video game championship, to which he had invited all comers. To my hyper-competitive brother Mark, this was an imperative, a chance to show the masses, or at least a few fellow vidiots, that his skills were the best, like Bruce Lee in *Enter the Dragon* or Jean-Claude Van Damme in *Bloodsport*.

Most kids are well-versed in video games today, but Mark's ravenous obsession with them when Day, in late 1982, put out the call for post-pinball wizards to come to Iowa made him mildly eccentric to his peers at school. While arcades nationwide were still flush with acned youth reeling from the insanity that was Pac-Man fever, only a select few, my brother among them, had come down with a bug so virulent that it was compelling them not just to spend entire Saturday afternoons plunking down quarters to play games with names like Bosconian, Xevious, and Zaxxon, but also to consider calling a total stranger hundreds of miles away to report their high scores. During these chats with Day, Mark would often make audacious declarations/threats typical of teenagers with type-A personalities, such as "What's the current high score on Bubbles? Oh, really? I can definitely beat that. You'll be hearing from me soon."

I wasn't at all surprised that he felt the need to turn video games into sport, as he had always been motivated by a desire to show others that he was the best. By contrast, while I loved playing video games with all of my soul, and constantly strived to improve my skills, even dutifully tracking my scores in a Detroit Tigers notebook, I felt that being able to play at all was its own reward. How Mark and I separately embraced the video game phenomenon illustrated a major difference between us that had first come to light when we'd begun collecting baseball cards a few years before. While I had mostly been content simply to own certain eye-pleasing baseball cards, even ones that had little value, such as my assemblage of twenty-seven worthless Jose Cruz–with-an-afro cards, Mark had set his sights on industry-wide domination: subscribing to the preeminent pricing guide to help him establish a figure for every item in his collection; renting tables at local card shows to sell the very sets he'd spent months amassing; and, ultimately, booking his own convention at the age of 14 in the faraway city of Detroit, for which he almost persuaded Hall of Fame slugger Johnny Mize to sign autographs. He was clearly operating on a different scale than I was.

But that was fine by me, as a fringe benefit of having an older brother whose drive to succeed at video games was greater than my own was that I was expected to tag along to provide him with moral support—which meant that I got to spend more time around wonderful, delicious video games.

Naturally, we knew where every machine within bike-riding distance was. A few times a week when we were both still attending the Christian Reform school, Mark and I would get off the bus, make a beeline for our bikes, and pedal furiously toward video game bliss. Sometimes this took us along a path through a cornfield near our house, where, emerging on the far side of the field and into a subdivision like Dorothy and the gang finally making it to Oz, we would eventually reach a convenience store that held, way in the back next to the bottle-redemption station, a rotating choice of two games. Initially the draw had been Asteroids, the 1979 space shoot-'em-up, concerning which Martin Amis, in his excellent nonfiction book *Invasion of the Space Invaders*, properly instructed, "Don't go mad and reduce the whole screen to rubble—you'll find yourself dodging bricks, and will be stoned to death like an Iranian rapist." But whatever game happened to be there—including lesser thrills like Jungle King, Moon Patrol, and Zoo Keeper—was fine by us. If it was Robotron: 2084 that we were seeking, we could make the perilous trek to 7-Eleven. We'd have to maneuver along a busy road without sidewalks or bike lanes, but more daunting by far was navigating around the hardscrabble teens who liked to congregate in the parking lot and spend time in the store's magazine section, where they would attempt to ogle copies of *Penthouse* and *Playboy* surreptitiously. It had all been worth the risk, however, once you were sucking on a Slurpee and standing at the controls, blasting mutated brain people. But by far my favorite of these bike-accessible destinations was the pizza place—and not only because the indigenous cuisine was super-tasty. The tiny restaurant held the immediate area's only Donkey Kong, my favorite game, and it was a sit-down machine, at that. Mark could sit on one side of the cabinet, and I could sit on the other, and we even had a built-in table to rest our pizza and Cokes on. If there was a heaven, I wanted that to be it.

But I knew the real reason that it was my preferred place to ride our bikes: I was better at Donkey Kong than my brother was. It could be both a joy and a source of personal shame to watch Mark play video games. He'd dominate his own personal favorites, spending hours at a time on them, often on a single quarter, attracting small throngs of inquisitive gamers who'd never seen such lofty scores or expertly accomplished moves. But quite often he would also make a point of schooling me on the titles I considered to be "mine." Few fraternal disappointments have been more crushing than when, after I'd spent two months seemingly mastering the video game adaptation of *Star Wars,* eventually claiming the highest rung on the game's leaderboard at our local arcade with a score of over three million points, he took an interest in the game and within two days had reached six million; worse, he then quit playing it because he claimed the game was too easy for him. But for some reason only the universe knows, he could never figure out how to beat me at Donkey Kong—and now that I think of it, that must be why we didn't go to the pizza place very often.

By the end of 1982, when Walter Day became a celebrity in our household, Mark and I—and even Matt, who was only five, yet could get to the banana level on Ms. Pac-Man!—had become regulars on the scene at various arcades around the city. The one downside to arcades was that going to them required getting a ride from one of our parents. What sucked about that was we'd have to fit it into their schedule; after they had completed whatever errand they had been running, it would be time to leave—even if you still had tokens. But man, the arcade: Upon entering any of these places, your first stop was always at the token machine to load up on a few handfuls of the local currency. Then, after buying a fountain Coke as big as your head, you'd wander off to survey the territories, which featured rows upon rows of blinking, blooping, intoxicating machines. I, for one, learned a lot about money management during my years of going regularly to the arcade. For example, if I had only twenty tokens, and our mom wouldn't be coming to pick us up for five hours, I would have to average fifteen minutes per game in order to avoid having to bum tokens off people. Being at an arcade with no money was like being a sex addict at a convent: You had to do a lot of talking if you wanted to get any play.

Thanks to his interaction with Twin Galaxies, Mark, with a handful of second- and third-best scores to his credit, had become a known commodity in the then-minuscule community of video game warriors. So, when Walter Day decided to stage the national video game championship, which would be taking place in January 1983, Mark was personally invited to come to Ottumwa to be one of the competitors—and the youngest of them, as well. Raising the stakes even more: *That's Incredible!*, a popular ABC series that documented the impressive feats of ordinary people (and which is now often conflated with NBC's similar offering, *Real People*), was going to be on hand to document the proceedings. If Mark managed to win the tournament, the entire world might conceivably know that he was the best video game player on the planet!

My dad, to his credit, understood the importance of this mission immediately. Staving off the minor objections of our mother and the thorny reality of how a man with no income would be able to pay for such an excursion, he had Mark and me and my brother's wide-eyed friend Steve—who cared little about video games but jumped at a chance to get away from his troubled home for a few days—in the car before dawn on the appointed day for the ten-hour drive to Ottumwa. The trip to Iowa, marking the first time I'd crossed the Mississippi, was the happiest four-day stretch that I ever spent in my dad's company. As hard as I try to remember anything bad about it, I can't. Even though the drive across hundreds of miles of completely flat terrain was interminable, and though the four of us shared a cramped, dingy hotel room, and though my dad snored, keeping us awake for the better part of three days, any minor quibbles were easily balanced out by getting to dine exclusively, to the delight of my pre-teen palate, at McDonald's. It was like going to Disney World, only better, because video games were the main attraction instead of stupid Goofy.

When we arrived in Ottumwa that afternoon, we convinced our dad to head straight for Twin Galaxies before we checked into our motel. The desire to see this video game Valhalla was almost an irrepressible signal, like the bizarre urges compelling Richard Dreyfuss in *Close Encounters of the Third Kind*. What we saw surprised us, though: The legendary arcade looked no different than any of the ones back in Grand Rapids, a mere mom-and-pop business whose address was literally on Main Street, U.S.A. I suppose I expected trumpets to blare and balloons to fall from the ceiling as we stepped inside, but none of that stuff happened. Still, it was no letdown. Because of its credentials, Twin Galaxies seemed to *matter,* as if the world were watching every time you popped a quarter into a machine.

For use in the tournament, Day had obtained a few games that had yet to be widely released—not just Pac-Man but Super Pac-Man, not just Donkey Kong but Donkey Kong Jr. To us, seeing these strange, new games in front of us was like telling a hungry alcoholic that he'd not only get more pie, but pie made out of alcohol. Day, a gregarious Willy Wonka type wearing a black-and-white striped referee's shirt, greeted us as we wandered goggle-eyed around the arcade, and Mark shook his hand as if he were the President. Later, after we'd gotten to play a few games, Day made a ceremonious announcement and went over the ground rules for the tournament, which was to begin promptly at ten a.m. the following morning. Mark and his fellow competitors would be tested on five different games, two of which were recently released titles that none of the participants could have played more than a few times. Each player would have five minutes to rack up as many points on each game as possible, and the scores would be added together to determine the top three finishers; this lucky trio would then be flown out to Hollywood to battle it out on the set of *That's Incredible!* Mark's jaw clenched and, based on experience, I knew this meant I wouldn't see him much during the rest of our time in Ottumwa. Grinding his teeth meant that he *had* to win one of these three slots, and that if I knew what was good for me, I would stay out of his way, unless he asked me to get him a Mountain Dew. Mark is one of the few people I've ever met who seems to have no fun while playing games; to him, winning is the only thing that matters, and the game itself is secondary. My dad, Steve, and I backed off and left him alone in the arcade for a few hours to practice, and we set off to check in to our motel a few blocks away and then eat Quarter Pounders. At the end of the night, Mark had to be physically dragged away from a game of Mad Planets, only grudgingly accepting the importance of sleep before a big day.

The town's quaint Main Street, which had been deathly quiet the previous afternoon, was buzzing on the morning of the tournament. Walter had managed to convince the mayor of Ottumwa to throw a parade in honor of the competitors, and as the four of us Michiganders approached the arcade, Mark was quickly ushered into a procession that also included a man outfitted in a gigantic Pac-Man suit. The streets were lined with Iowans bundled in winter coats and sporting bad haircuts; I figured many of them had turned up more out of curiosity about why their town had attracted all this attention than out of any genuine interest in the reason behind the parade—or, given that many parade-goers were clustered near the ABC camera crew on hand, maybe they'd come because they were hoping to get on national television. Either way, the excitement and crowd from the parade spilled over into Twin Galaxies and made for a tense, hot competitive arena, almost as if it had become Thunderdome.

The tournament would take place over two days; my big

concern was that spectators who managed to squeeze into Twin Galaxies were expressly forbidden from playing any games themselves while the tournament was going on. Furthermore, because we weren't close enough to the screens to see how particular players were faring, it became clear pretty much immediately that this was not going to be fun for me or Steve for very long. After an hour of watching teenager after teenager with really bad skin intensely focus on a game I'd never played before, and with Mark huddled nervously in a far corner looking like he was about to puke up fireballs, Steve and I asked my dad if we could go across the street to a rival arcade so that we could actually play some games ourselves. "You want to play Konkey Donk, don't you?" asked my dad. Ignoring our laughter, he reached into his pocket and mysteriously pulled out a few dollars, which he split evenly between Steve and me. "Spend it all in one place!" he joked.

He stayed behind to provide moral support for Mark while Steve and I went across the street to the second arcade. It's difficult to fathom, but in 1983, there were arcades everywhere; even a small municipality like Ottumwa was able to support two, and there had been at least seven that we knew of in the Grand Rapids area. And the one across from Twin Galaxies was also bustling. Being two years older, Steve announced as soon as we entered the doors that he was going to play Skee-Ball, which I took to mean that he was going to check out the girls who were playing it—and his departure was to my benefit. Solitude would be vital, as I was looking to stage a tournament of my own inside these walls: me vs. me on the fields of Donkey Kong. For some reason, more than any other video game I had ever played, I *got* Donkey Kong. I had played it so often and studied it so closely that it was almost like I knew how Mario breathed. Given how passionate I was about it, I probably should have considered going into carpentry, or something involving ladders or jumping over barrels. And there, in a back row of cabinets at this second, seedier arcade, far from the watching eyes of my brother, Walter Day, or a television film crew, sat the cabinet I was seeking. This Donkey Kong machine was almost daring me to shove a dozen quarters into its coin slot. Five games in, I hit a groove and eclipsed my highest previous score. Soon after, I made it to the fourth pie factory, a good five screens farther than I'd ever gone before. I finished this magic game—one I've never come close to duplicating since—with a score of 266,400. It was exhilarating.

Ironically, although we were here in support of my brother's quest for fame, I was certain that my score was a world record; I had memorized it from the issue of a video game magazine we'd bought for the drive to Iowa. The feeling in my stomach as I looked at the screen, scarcely believing the score myself, must have been the same that a fringe minor league baseball player gets upon being told he's being promoted to The Show. And for once, I wanted the world to know. I found Steve and told him to guard the machine with his life, or at least with his fists, and I bolted across the street to tell Walter Day about my score. Fighting through the crowd, I passed my dad and told him, loudly, what had just occurred. He made a facial gesture like he'd just seen a Republican get hit over the head with a fake hammer—he didn't know whether to be happy or not. I moved on, squeezing toward the rear of the arcade, where Walter Day was judging the tournament. As I emerged into the area where the competition was being held, I gathered myself so that I might present my score to Day as calmly as possible—that is, like a true champion. And then I looked up and saw, hanging high above the crowd, something I'd somehow missed before: the official video game scoreboard. It listed, in Magic Marker, the current high scores on many major games; to my eternal dismay, the score posted for Donkey Kong was above 800,000. It was confusing and a bit embarrassing, like being told your zipper's down, because I could have sworn that the magazine I'd read on the way down had printed a number lower than the one I'd tallied across the street. It was in this way that I learned about magazine lead times—the printed record had been a few months old, eons in the annals of video game scores. I had merely broken a sad, old record.

It was probably for the best, too, considering that it would have taken the spotlight off Mark in his shiningest hour, especially considering that the tournament didn't exactly lead Mark to the video game glory he'd been dreaming of. He finished 14th out of 19; to add further insult, he was edited out of the related footage that appeared a few weeks later on *That's Incredible!* (Oddly enough, Steve and I appeared on the show, standing front and center in a staged crowd shot taken through the window of Twin Galaxies.) To have been able to lord a world record over him during the long ride home would have made for, I'm guessing, an even longer ride home. Still, given that he was the youngest competitor in the tournament, it was a magnificent showing—far better than my piddly Donkey Kong score. But it's all been downhill for me from there.

For his part, my dad acted like a hero in Ottumwa. The entire trip he was one-hundred-percent supportive, cheering Mark on and buying him double cheeseburgers to ease the pain of defeat. Some dads we encountered through Little League seemed bent on pressuring their kids to succeed; my dad never cared whether we hit a home run or struck out pathetically, so long as we had a good time playing. If the Ottumwa trip illuminated one thing,* it was that my dad wasn't as bad as he looked on paper.

As I sat inside the screen door, talking with my dad and thinking about how this trip to the swamp was, like Ottumwa, not so bad, I realized that my dad's low-pressure approach to parenting was part of what had made the day enjoyable. My dad hadn't cared whether Mark had become a video game champion; similarly, he wasn't hoping that I'd end up becoming an intrepid outdoorsman who could kill his own supper and cook it over a fire. He just wanted me to relish the adventure, as always.

His lack of pushing in my childhood had meant that I was able to set my own goals, which in turn sometimes led me to pursue them more intensely than I might have cared to had I been trying to live up to someone else's expectations.

---

* Actually, that video game vacation also demonstrated another thing: That my dad was, as ever, hilariously clueless. At the end of the trip, we dropped off Steve, who lived a few minutes' drive from our house. My dad pulled our two-door hatchback into the driveway of Steve's home, and we all just sat there for a full fifteen seconds. Finally, my dad looked into the rearview mirror at Steve, who was sitting directly behind him, and asked, "Can you get out?" Steve replied, "Yeah, if you open the door." My dad had somehow forgotten that, in order for a rear-seat passenger to exit, he would have to move his seat forward and unlatch the driver's side door.

But as we talked idly to each other that evening in Hillsdale, I found myself uncharacteristically creating my own expectations, feeling determined to make a success out of this venture even though no one else, especially not my dad, was judging the proceedings. Noticing this happening—and realizing that I was not Mark, that my dad wasn't Walter Day, and that snakes weren't video games—I sat back and tried to put all thoughts of missions and objectives out of my head. It was harder than I thought it would be. Maybe my dad did have a thing or two to teach me, after all.

EIGHT

As enjoyable as trading old stories had been, it was after ten p.m., and the long day of travel and activity had left me feeling exhausted. Plus, I was homesick. I know that's not a burly, mountain man thing to admit, but there you have it. So, I begged free of my dad and went to look for my cell phone so that I could call Megan, whom I had been dating for roughly a year. After briefly cleaning up in the cabin's bare-bones bathroom, I shut the door to my room, relieved to finally have some privacy. I fished around in my bag for the shockingly primitive cell phone, dialed Megan's number, and then . . . call failed. There seemed to be no cellular service whatsoever in this part of Hillsdale County, something I hadn't bargained on. It was another jarring reminder that I was in the middle of nowhere, and that I really *was* alone with my dad. For a second, I contemplated commandeering the Subaru and driving back to the surely reception-rich Jackson, so that I could rehash the day with

Megan—and assure her that I hadn't been eaten by some sort of swamp sucker—but instead I heaved the phone back into my suitcase with disgust.

I turned my thoughts to the positives. As I settled back onto the queen-size bed for a well-deserved night's sleep, I reveled in the Posturepedic goodness of the surprisingly comfortable mattress. Above, a ceiling fan whirred rhythmically and circulated the stuffy June air around the room. Outside, there wasn't a sound being made except for the soothing chirp of crickets and the gentle summer wind. A half hour or so later, I was just about to fall into the soundest sleep of my life when it started: my dad's impossibly loud snoring. Even though I had known all too well about his habit of making power-saw-like sounds while asleep, I had foolishly thought a closed door between our rooms would block it out. But it appeared that I should have traveled with my own soundproofing equipment, or at the very least, airport-tarmac-worker earmuffs.

I contemplated going out into the living room, where my dad was dozing like a hibernating bear, and setting about rifling through kitchen drawers just loudly enough to wake him. But then I remembered that when I was a kid, my dad used to play a game with us called Sleeping Giant. In this game, he would pretend to be asleep and lie there unmoving as Mark and I attempted to sneak up on him. When one of us got close to his reclining form on the bed, he would sit up with a start, yell, "Who dares wake the sleeping giant?" and then leap from the bed to chase us down the hall with a terrifying roar. This was a game I had no interest in reprising tonight—and frankly, even the memory scares me. But as I have learned, there are worse things dads can do in their sleep than snore.

Given my dad's odd behavior and the state of our house when I was growing up, an invitation to stay at a friend's home felt like the equivalent of drawing a "get out of jail free" card in Monopoly. But sometimes I'd get all excited about a chance to see how the more normal half lived only to discover that my friends had their own weird parents to deal with. One night when I was ten, I was lying on the floor in my friend Ben's living room, one of several boys tucked into sleeping bags so that our heads converged and our feet extended out from the center like the petals of a sunflower. It was Ben's tenth birthday, and we were all there for a sleepover, even my brother, who had jealously protested about my privilege and had my mom wrangle his invitation. But the sleepover was actually pretty dull. That is, until midnight, when Ben announced that he had thought of something awesomely fun for us to do. He asked us to pay attention while he laid out the plan for our exciting, covert operation; we'd have to follow it to the letter if we hoped to succeed. He had to speak softly because just around the corner his mother and stepdad were asleep in the master bedroom with the door open.

"The objective," said Ben, revealing our mission, "is to get the T-shirt hanging on the exercise bike on the other side of my mom's bed."

Ben traced a map of the master bedroom as if he was laying out a battle plan, preparing troops who were about to venture behind enemy lines. The seriousness with which he did this was particularly ludicrous, given that earlier that

night the five of us had already been in there to avail ourselves of the house's only TV. It was a large, sunken room
with earth-toned shag carpeting throughout. To get to the
exercise bike, we'd have to round the corner to the open
bedroom door, navigate through a short entryway, then
crawl down a step, silently creep about five feet to the foot
of the king-size waterbed, and then walk around the foot
of the bed to the bike. And then, obviously, we'd have to
come back out to the living room with shirt in hand—all
completely unnoticed. Making matters more difficult, Ben's
mom had a notoriously bad temper, and as we all knew, a
serious potty mouth. His stepdad, Dennis, was a large fellow, standing only five feet, eight inches, but weighing in at
what looked like 300 pounds. As I sat there listening to Ben
rally the troops, it seemed to me there was a good chance
this game could go horribly awry. It also seemed like the best
thing anyone had ever thought of.

One by one, with Ben leading the charge, we crawled
on our bellies into the room like ants filing up the side of
a picnic basket—apart from the reality that ants would be
going after sustenance, not something as inconsequential as a
ratty workout shirt that probably smelled like old sweat. At
first, none of us could make it past the step; the insanity of
the situation dawned on each of us at this carpeted Maginot
Line, and we'd have to shimmy quickly back out to the living room to laugh off a case of the giggles. But after a few
steadily bold attempts, Ben managed to make it to the foot of
the bed. I had fought back the laughter myself and was right
behind him, in the five-foot no-man's-land between the step
and the bed. He turned around and gave me a thumbs-up,

a premature gesture of "mission accomplished" that would rival President George W. Bush's speech aboard an aircraft carrier to proclaim "victory" in Iraq.

Right about then, however, Dennis sat bolt upright in the bed and, in a loud, low voice that made me think he was addressing us, he said, "I wish I had a sack of potatoes."

Now, this is probably the funniest non sequitur that anyone could ever utter when fully awake. Mix in the fact that Dennis was sound asleep and that, unbeknownst to him, his stepson and three young strangers were engaged in a ridiculous mission at the foot of his bed, and it was too much for any of us to bear. We each bit the carpet to stifle an avalanche of laughter.

But after a weighty pause of five seconds, he added, almost regretfully, "I should have had a sack of potatoes."

I had no choice but to stand up and run back to the living room to laugh, and I couldn't stop for at least five minutes. My brother looked like he was dying, doubled over and unable to contain his response to the hilarity we'd just witnessed. Ben, who also emerged on his belly from the bedroom, was beet red from stifling laughter. This is the origin of my theory that there is nothing funnier than a fat man in boxer briefs sitting up and reciting variations on a phrase involving potatoes.

But we still hadn't gotten the shirt! And now we were about a half hour into the endeavor with no results. If we quit the mission now, we would go down in history as total failures. So we resumed our race-crawling to the exercise bike and just hoped to hell Dennis wouldn't sit up and say anything. Mark could never make it more than a few inches beyond the door before having to go outside to laugh at the memory of the quote. Ben, who had the most to lose, was also the boldest. And, it would turn out, the stupidest. He made it to the bike while I was at the foot of the bed and grabbed the shirt, but it got caught on the handlebars. As the shirt snapped back, it grazed his mom's bare leg on the bed.

We both made a break for the living room, and the others figured out what they had to do based on the look on Ben's face. On cue, we all pretended to be asleep.

As we had most feared, his mother stomped out of the bedroom. She yelled, "You little shits—don't pretend to be asleep. I know you were in there!" We lost all pretense of feigning sleep and watched incredulously as she turned to take out her rage on Ben. "You little shit." Each word was said simultaneously with a kick to his behind. You. *Kick.* Little. *Kick.* Shit. *Kick.* Mark and I were laughing uproariously at this bizarre example of parental discipline, but we were also completely scandalized—our mother would never use a four-letter word, much less kick us while using one. Yet for some reason, this low-level brutality was even funnier than the potatoes quote. Our laughter made Ben's mom even madder, and she kicked him even harder. You. *Kick.* Will. *Kick.* Never. *Kick.* Have. *Kick.* Friends. *Kick.* Over. *Kick.* Again. *Kick.* The strangest part of this entire scene was that Ben was simultaneously laughing hysterically and screaming in pain, which produced a sound not unlike a starving tomcat or Paris Hilton in heat.

The next morning, I woke up staring at an unfamiliar wood ceiling. For a moment, my sleep-addled brain was confused by the presence of the ceiling fan above me. In Brooklyn, I was renting the ground floor of a two-family house owned by a family whose kitchen was directly above my bed. Much of the patriarch's extended family lived with them, including a toddler, who literally could not walk quietly. Another grandchild liked to bounce basketballs on the wood floor. There was no rug upstairs, either, so the screeches from chairs around their eat-in-kitchen's table could be heard whenever they moved. On top of all that, they were insanely early risers. The only reason I'd lived there for so long was that the rent was an absolute steal for the neighborhood. Once I'd realized where I was—or rather, where I was not—it felt nice to wake up away from the usual noise.

But getting up today also came with the knowledge that a bigger challenge was in store for me—as my dad described it, "heavy swamping." We'd be hiking through thick woods to a much larger swamp a few miles away from our cabin, which, when my dad had last checked in 1991, had been teeming with copperbellies. More than anything, my dad wanted to see these snakes thriving like they were in the good old days. Last night, while he was cooling off on the porch and sipping from his plastic cup of wine from a box, I had asked him why he felt the need to attempt such a strenuous hike at this stage of his life. Given his age and generally poor physical condition, it had definitely seemed risky to me. He had answered by saying, "I just like to see if they're okay, you know?"

When I came out into the living room, my dad asked me if I wanted any coffee, a beverage that he deliberately pronounced as "kyaw-fee." I'd certainly need some caffeine to get pepped up for our hike, but I immediately noticed his pants and found myself speechless. They had a camouflage pattern on the front and were made of blue denim in the back; they were the mullet of trousers. My dad called them "country camos" and explained that they're the most comfortable swamping pants he owned. I called them "embarrassing and weird" but was silently grateful that we were unlikely to be spotted by other humans, much less fashionable ones, while he was sporting this getup.

I regained my sense of purpose and accepted a cup of piping hot coffee. It was Folger's Crystals, which, despite all of the commercials I recalled proving the contrary, did not fool my coffee-snob palate for one minute. I took the cup and set off for the bathroom to get ready for the long day ahead, but when I turned on the faucet, the water stayed cold. After a minute, I groaned in frustration and stormed out to the living room to ask my dad how long I'd have to wait for the water to heat up.

"I was going to tell you about that . . . ," he said, without looking at me.

Because the house had gone unused for a few weeks, the water heater had been shut off when we arrived. When my dad had woken up, he'd gone down to the basement to turn the water on; in the process, he had inadvertently broken off a knob on the water heater. Translation: There would be no hot water for showers, which was not what a guy waking up smelling of swamp stink wanted to hear. "Could be worse," my dad mused, irritatingly. As I offered to go down to the basement to take a look and see if the water heater could be fixed, he told me not to bother and tried to deflect blame from himself, convinced there was prior need for repair. "It's happened before," he said. "It had to."

I walked out onto the porch in disgust. At least there I could drink my terrible cup of coffee in peace and feel like I was preserving some semblance of a morning wake-up routine. The thought occurred to me: I had no idea why I had come on this trip. Sure, I had come here, in part, to experience my dad's lifelong obsession, but now the endeavor was starting to feel like a boring, belated Take Your Child to Work Day. All of the frustrating memories I had from childhood were playing themselves out again in front of me. *It's happened before. It had to.* Indeed.

As I sipped my cup of foul swill and seethed while looking out at the lake, I saw a muskrat swimming in the water. Because I had nothing else to look at, I watched it as it went to shore, collected some branches, and brought them back out to a little hut it was building. My dad slid the door open and joined me out on the porch, where he began watching the muskrat, too. Neither of us said anything; we just observed the industrious critter following his instincts to set himself up for survival. It was fascinating that he knew exactly what to do. As a human with a supposedly more developed brain, I suddenly felt embarrassed that I wouldn't know how to build my own house unless someone gave me a massive instruction booklet and a team of engineers to decipher it. Watching the muskrat reminded me that there were fascinating things worth learning about out here in the wilderness, and that I'd volunteered to discover what they were. So despite my unshowered, pissed-off state, I downed the rest of my coffee and said to my dad, "Okay, I'm ready."

Soon, I was watching my dad stride confidently down a country lane leading away from the house, and it became clear to me that he had been drawn to nature because of the solitude. Sure, it was hot, even at ten a.m., but the plus side was that there was no one around. The only noises I heard were coming from us, the wind, the birds, and the bullfrogs. As a resident of Brooklyn, New York's most populous and surely noisiest borough, I found the quiet to be nice. But this was my dad's comfort zone, not mine. I would never become acclimated enough to the outdoors to feel at home here the way he seemed to be. Trudging down a gravel road to an even more remote swamp in search of reptiles wasn't a relaxing endeavor for me, but it did relax my dad. He couldn't wait to plunge farther into the woods, while my thoughts kept drifting toward showers.

We came across a roadside lake, after Cellars Road had passed by a sign that said ROUGH ROAD AHEAD and promptly turned into a walking path. The road itself used to be open, but my dad had rallied some conservationists to shut it down in 1992. Applying '60s-style activism to an environmental effort, my dad considered this to be his greatest professional achievement, and regularly thought proudly about the snakes that'd been spared from deadly encounters with vehicles because of what he had done. The path ran for about a half mile here before meeting up with the dirt road on the other side of a bridge that it used to be connected to. Residents on both sides of this broken stretch of Cellars Road have complained that they now must drive around three sides of a square to get to the opposite point, whereas their commute could be cut in half if the bridge was still operational; they weren't at all concerned that the bridge ran over a stream that my dad said was "the snake highway."

Copperbellies have long been labeled as water snakes, but it turns out that's a bit of a misnomer. One of my dad's most surprising discoveries was that their habitat was not precisely rivers and lakes, but also swamps and woodlands, which partially explained why they weren't being found for so many years. And that information worried him. Because copperbellies regularly travel between deep-woods swamps alongside or through the streams in this area, many had slithered out onto the flat surface of the road running through their habitat here to bask in the sun or, literally, to cross the road. When cars had been allowed to use the bridge, the result was DORs galore. He was proud that the threat, at least here, had been eliminated, and he hoped it would help preserve the local snake population for years to come.

The bridge, my dad said, was up ahead, but first we walked by a small, unimpressive lake filled with cattails and lily pads. It also contained a real beaver lodge, which was something I'd never seen with my own eyes and figured was a thing only found in nature programs. As we walked, I could hear frogs and other unknown animals jumping into the water, disturbed by our presence. I asked my dad if he'd ever waded out into this particular lake. "Of course," he said, matter-of-factly. "You have to." However, because there weren't any trees surrounding the lake, and copperbellies preferred woodlands, it was highly unlikely that we'd find any of them here, my dad explained. And so into the woods we went.

A few minutes beyond the lake, we arrived at the creaky

old iron bridge. Once there, my dad asked if we could stop and rest, although it might have been that he wanted to commune. Many flies buzzed about, causing a bit of inborn agitation in my gut, but whatever—I allowed him the moment. At that point, I hadn't found any of our trekking to be physically challenging, but I could see that it was putting a mild strain on my dad, and so, no matter the reason, I was happy to oblige him. It didn't hurt that we'd stopped above a narrow, sun-dappled creek out of an issue of *Field & Stream*. It was the perfect place to gather strength for what was ahead. After several minutes' rest, my dad indicated that he was ready to go, and I almost felt disappointed to be moving on after such a pleasant stop. The walk from the bridge continued along the former road, and after what felt like just a few more minutes, we reached a stretch of the path that seemed completely arbitrary to me. But my dad stopped and said, "Here we are!" Without further ceremony, he entered the dense scrub brush at the side of the road and disappeared from my sight. Taking a deep breath and clutching my walking stick for dear life, I followed him. I knew there would be no Turkish delight waiting for me on the other side, but entering the brush gave the eerie feeling that I was going into the wardrobe.

Once we made it through, we were surrounded by a dense stand of swamp trees. The canopy almost completely blocked the daylight. This particular swamp, approximately the size of a football field, had mostly dried up, and the ground was littered with dead trees. It was also crazy with mud. My dad explained that this wasn't technically a swamp, as it wasn't self-sustaining; it was an area that flooded as precipitation accumulated and snow melted, and which gave way to dry dirt as summer progressed. As I made my way across the muddy expanse, often stepping into sticky muck (which embarrassingly, made my face scrunch in disgust, as if I were stepping into a bucket of sloppy joes), I realized how much effort my dad must have expended back when he visited places like this regularly. It was tough work just walking one hundred yards. So I was relieved when I noticed a clearing ahead, maybe a quarter mile away, past some green shrubs and trees that seemed to denote the end of the swamp area. Light was coming through their leaves, pleasantly indicating that the swamp came equipped with an emergency exit.

After navigating through the dried-out swamp and breaking through the shrub barrier, we hit upon a small path, moderately more well-lit, that my dad said had been formed by deer, and sure enough, I could see tell-tale hoof prints. "Watch for ticks!" said my dad. I wasn't exactly sure how one was supposed to watch for insects the size of the head of a pin, but I definitely didn't want one of them getting on me. When my dad had first started feeling the pain in his right shoulder, his doctor initially diagnosed the problem as Lyme disease. There is nothing good about Lyme disease, including its name, which, despite referring to a town in Connecticut, conjures up deceptive images of citrus drinks by the pool. The weird disease affects the nervous system, and in addition to arthritis-like joint symptoms, can afflict its victim with unusual behavior, along the lines of the DTs or mild dementia. (On second thought, maybe my dad *did* have Lyme disease.) At any rate, I wanted no part of a disease borne by bugs.

Soon the path spilled out into a field, and I could breathe again. There had been so many unknown, potentially hazardous elements on all sides of me that I'd experienced a kind of claustrophobia. Being in a wide-open space again was momentarily calming. But then the biting flies descended on me like smart bombs and the calm disappeared. I hadn't been bitten yet, due to my heavy clothing and the DEET, but there was always the worry that one would get through my defenses. We began walking up a slight incline through a field of daisies and Queen Anne's lace, and toads and crickets hopped in front of us. It was a pastoral scene that reminded me of spending time with my dad at the farm in Saranac. There had been a steep hill running up behind the house, rising some five hundred feet—my dad called the summit "the top of the world." It was a grueling climb even for an energetic youngster to get to the summit. Yet my dad took us there often to watch the sunset. I didn't like the climb. And truth be told, I didn't even like sitting up there interminably, as he smoked cigarettes, pipes, or, I'm sure, joints, and pointed out useless constellations, when there was perfectly good spaghetti to eat at home, and cards to be dealt. But the walk down was a riot, especially when you ran. You'd almost literally fly, the hill was so steep, and you felt like the fastest person in the world, like the Flash, only without the skintight red suit. It was as if you were barreling down a mountain; you were both in control and completely out of control at the same time. Evading thorny blackberry vines and swerving around tricky corners, for the most part letting gravity do its thing, you'd finally emerge through the cluster of fir trees directly behind the house, and soon be rejoicing in its climate-controlled embrace.

We came over the crest of the hill and soon got to a wall of brambles. I carefully used my walking stick to push the vines aside, holding them for my dad, and we made our way through, slowly but surely, to another dark place, this one cloaked under a thick canopy of birch trees. And there it was: a bona fide swamp, much bigger than the one from the previous evening, and more like the quagmires I had imagined, sans the psychotic drifters. Or so I hoped.

As I believe I have discussed, I had seen enough movies to have been terrified that, in a place like this, a maniac with a machete could pop out at us out of nowhere. It was an irrational fear, but if either of these things were to happen, my dad and I would have been screwed. I mean, there was nowhere to go. We could have hidden behind trees, maybe, and hoped our attacker gave up quickly. But there was no way we could have climbed a tree—the lowest branches were ten feet above us, and we weren't koalas. About the only thing we could have considered was wading deep into the middle of the swamp and diving under the water, using a reed to breathe like they did in ninja movies. But then, taking movies literally was what had me spooked in the first place.

A baseless thought oddly rumbled through my head that if we were to get lost out here, my dad and I would have to hug to conserve our body heat. Our branch of the Sellers family wasn't big on hugging—I can't think of a single instance of my parents hugging, or a time in my childhood when they hugged us. And so, in our collective opinion, there are very few instances where touching is acceptable, or even necessary. But being stranded in the middle of nowhere with the threat of freezing to death would certainly be one of them. Luckily, it was still 80 degrees out—no huddling required.

The main area of the swamp appeared to be oblong in shape, surrounded by short, scraggly trees. From where we stood, I could see out into the center of the swamp; bright sunshine was pouring down on a healthy number of bushes that were growing on an island in the midst of the pond, some thirty feet from the edge. My dad explained that the island was likely to be the big snake habitat in this area and that he would have to take a slightly circuitous route to get a closer look because the dense vegetation that ringed the shores of the swamp blocked easier access. I still didn't feel up to joining him in swamp wading, but I offered my proven snake-spotting skills in trade. "Good," said my dad, removing his glasses and wiping his brow. "I could use your eyes."

We walked around the perimeter of the swamp, where my dad proceeded to set up shop on a log where, he explained, his vantage point would allow him a chance to see if a copperbelly just happened to swim by. My dad's approach to spotting the object of his reptilian fascination had become more meditative and philosophical as he'd aged. And waiting on a log for snakes was an activity that suited him perfectly. After fifteen minutes of contemplation, he suddenly stood up and announced that he was going to wade out into the middle of the swamp. Walking deliberately to the shore, he took a first tentative step into the water and began moving forward confidently, if very slowly. All the while he was talking. As he advanced, he gave me the play-by-play, but didn't raise his voice as he got farther out into the middle. Soon he was standing thigh-high in the stagnant water forty-five feet away from me, and all I could pick out was a line about "submergent vegetation."

I remained on dry land at the edge of the swamp, occasionally surveying the water for snakes myself. When I looked up, I could no longer see my dad, although I could still hear his indecipherable babbling. He reappeared in my field of vision a few minutes later, poking the trees on the island with his stick. After a few stabs with his stick, he turned and headed toward me. He emerged from the swamp looking tired, wet, and not a little disappointed.

"Well, they're not here," he said, and sat back on the log to smoke a cigarette.

After my dad took his last drag and had caught his breath, he explained that there was one more place to check, this one even farther into the woods. He led the charge along a washed-out ravine and up a slight incline. I found it tough to navigate because I had to lift my legs over fallen branches repeatedly and step over and in small streams of water. After a half hour of mostly silent walking, we finally reached the next swamp, smaller than the one we'd just visited, but bigger than the swamp from the previous day. This was the swamp that led to my dad's getting his first survey grant. In 1983, he took a group of officials from the Department of Natural Resources here; they needed to verify the existence of a live copperbelly before rubber-stamping his assignment. After a long day of a fruitless search through three separate swamps, and right after the skeptical officials had announced they had to leave, my dad spotted something in the water. "There," he said, pointing. It was the first proof of the presence of a live copperbelly officially recorded in nearly twenty years.

Without delay, my dad waded out into the middle of the water expectantly, but after a half hour of nosing around, he came back to shore, looking even more dejected. Once again, he hadn't seen any snakes. This was disappointing. So far, in our two days here, we had seen only two copperbellies, both tiny. We had found little evidence that the thriving population my dad had fought so hard to protect was still thriving.

It was four p.m., and even though I hadn't been wading in the swamps like my dad had, I felt exhausted. I wanted a shower—even a cold one—and a nap. I wanted to call my girlfriend. I wanted to go home. The same couldn't be said for my dad, who seemed reluctant to leave without seeing a snake. But when I pointed out that it was a long way back to the cabin, he looked at me and said, "I just can't do anymore today. I hope that's okay." I rejoiced inwardly, but told him that that would be fine. But as we headed back toward the house through the same thickets and mud puddles we'd passed earlier, I noticed that he was struggling. He was out of breath, and his legs were wobbling like they were made of rubber. I commanded him to sit down on a fallen tree and gave him some water from my canteen.

Despite the fact that he'd had two minor heart attacks and just three years prior to this snake trek had suffered a bout with congestive heart failure that had caused his body to hold so much water that he literally ballooned up from retention until he resembled a cross between my dad and Louie Anderson, he was a man who had always exuded confidence during walks in the woods. But I realized that I had let his desire to show me what he used to do and where he'd found the snakes get the better of my assessment of his physical well-being; he was huffing and puffing even after we'd sat on the log for ten minutes, his body language suggesting that someone had stuck a pin in him and let out all the air. We stayed on the dead tree until his breath returned, and I told him that we could just take our time getting back. We slowly navigated back through the brambles and the field and the deer path and, finally, with relative ease, we reached the disused portion of Cellars Road. By the time we made it to the driveway leading to the cabin, it was nearly five p.m. Even by my marginally more physically capable standards, it had been a long day. My dad must have truly been exhausted.

As we approached the cabin, we noticed a pickup truck parked in the driveway. A tanned and burly man, probably in his early fifties, looked up from some lawn equipment and nodded in our direction. He seemed surprisingly unfazed by the sight of two sweaty, dirty men walking straight toward him.

"Hi, Mark," he called out. As we got closer to him, I noticed that he was wearing a T-shirt bearing the slogan BEAUTY IS IN THE EYE OF THE BEER HOLDER. "How's the cabin treating you?"

My dad said hello and introduced me—it was the man who owned the cabin. My dad thanked him for letting us crash here and said the place had been wonderful so far, conveniently leaving out the part about the busted water heater. I listened to them talk for a moment about snakes—or the lack of them—and then begged off to head inside to change out of my sweat-soaked swamp gear. It felt good to sit down after the long day we'd had, and I wondered if my dad shouldn't be inside lying down after our exhausting trek. I considered going outside and insisting that he rest, but something told me that ordering my dad around would not be the best way to get him to comply. If my dad had enjoyed following orders, he might have led a very different life. After I'd stripped off my socks and let some of the sweat of the day evaporate, I went out to the porch to check on my dad. I opened the door and saw the pickup truck accelerating out of the driveway, kicking up gravel. My dad walked slowly toward the house.

"You didn't tell him about the water heater, did you?" I asked.

"Best to wait until we're gone," he replied, and snickered, as though this were some accepted rule of staying at other people's houses that everyone knew. Or as though a hot shower was not at all necessary for someone who had just waded through a muck-filled swamp. I laughed bitterly, walked back inside, and took the best freezing cold shower of my life.

The next morning, I awoke to the sounds of my dad rummaging around in the front room. Slowly pulling myself together, I was dismayed to learn that my legs and back were completely sore from the previous day's unfamiliar activity. I would have literally killed a man to have been able to take a hot shower or even wash my face with a warm towel. Instead, I was staring down another day—luckily, the final one we had planned—of walking around in moderate levels of filth and lathering myself up with bug spray.

On the plus side, I was actually contemplating entering the water myself today. It had occurred to me as I'd dozed off that I hadn't been getting quite as involved in this project as I'd originally intended. The idea, of course, had been to get a better understanding of my dad. Walking the swamps with him and seeing where he caught the snakes had given me the visual picture I'd lacked all these years, and it would help place the stories he always told about important moments in his life in a real setting. And I was certainly tired and sore enough to appreciate how difficult his chosen line of work had actually been. But even my dad's girlfriend, Tina, had once entered the swamp with him. I was just being a baby.

With that in mind, I limped confidently out to the living room to inform my dad of my new resolve. But when I saw my dad, he was sitting on the edge of the prison-grade bunk bed he'd been crashing on just off the kitchen, and looking at the floor.

"Dad, are you okay?" I asked. "What's up?"

He looked up at me and smiled. "Yeah, I'm fine," he said. "Just a little tired. And sore. And bald. Pretty lucky to be alive, though." This last part of the quote, a lyric from a Bob Dylan song, made me laugh—even while exhausted, he was still goofy.

I knew that in his heart he wanted to stay and finish what we'd come here to do: document a thriving community of copperbelly water snakes. But I could tell that there was something more behind his wiped-out demeanor. It was clear that my resolve to enter the water with him had arrived a day too late. My dad was in rough shape and I knew I needed to get him home. While our snake survey definitely hadn't been a success, if my dad wound up in the hospital it would have gone down as an absolute disaster.

And so instead of telling him about my decision to enter the water—a revelation that I suspected would have been so thrilling to him that it would have kept him in the swamp all day, despite better judgment—I schemed a way to get him to safety. "You're not going to like this, Dad, but I was wondering if it would be okay if we just went home?" I asked. "My legs are really tired and I'm not sure I'm up for another day of this."

He eyed me curiously. On the one hand, he was well aware that I would like nothing better than a quality shower, and he obviously knew from long experience that the slog through the woods yesterday likely could have sapped my energy. On the other hand, my voice might have betrayed my altruistic motive. But he took the question for what it was. "Boom," he said. "Let's went."

After packing the car slowly and dropping the keys off at the owner's farm nearby, we began the two-hour drive toward Grand Rapids, where I would be staying for a few days before returning to Brooklyn. As we drove back over rolling hills on our way out of Hillsdale County, my dad came to a conclusion: "I think it's time to hang up my swamp sneakers."

NINE

Less then a month after returning from our swamp expedition, my dad went into cardiac arrest while being administered a routine stress test at his cardiologist's office.

He had been getting these tests, which typically involved walking on an inclined treadmill with heart monitors attached to his chest, without much incident since his heart trouble had started roughly twenty years ago. I say "without much incident" because the tests were invariably accompanied by my dad's skepticism about doctors and his dislike for being poked and prodded. But this time was different.

As soon as I found out, I couldn't help but think that I had pushed my dad too hard on our trip; insisting on leaving the swamp a day early hadn't been enough. But even more upsetting was the fact that I didn't even find out about what had happened at the doctor's office until several weeks *after* it had occurred. I have only recently put a significant effort into reconnecting with my dad, and vice versa—but it turned out that we were as yet not close enough for him to share important health information with me immediately. And although we had exchanged a flurry of self-congratulatory recaps of our trip immediately after returning, I hadn't bothered to check in with him about his health since resuming my snake-free Brooklyn life. He had seemed to be okay when we'd parted ways in Grand Rapids, and his notes to me had been upbeat. His struggles on our last hike had nearly evaporated from my mind. So when the news hit, arriving in the form of a lengthy, impersonal e-mail, I was stunned by just how precarious my dad's health had become.

"I got on the treadmill and almost immediately had trouble just walking on it because it moved fast and from the start was slanted uphill," he explained. "Still, I tried to keep up for five minutes, but it was a struggle throughout and I said, 'How much longer?'"

His hamstrings had fatigued and his legs had nearly given out. His mouth and throat had been dry, and he had been having trouble breathing. The technicians who were assisting with the test had taken him off the treadmill and made him lie down. They told him his heart had been racing too fast.

"Next thing I knew," he wrote, "besides having a very hot, burning head after some kinda magnesium injection, the EMT arrived. The techs said I was going to the emergency room."

He was taken by ambulance to a hospital twenty minutes away, in downtown Grand Rapids, where he was put in a bed in the emergency room. He stayed awake through it all. They diagnosed the problem as ventricular tachycardia, a condition that causes the heart to race at more than one hundred beats per minute.

"They shocked my heart with electric paddles or something," he wrote. "I was knocked out on an anesthetic during that process." When he came to, the hospital staff recommended that he have an atrial defibrillator implanted into his shoulder, with wires running into his left ventricle. "I said I was not ready to buy the thirty-thousand-dollar operation yet and would get back to them," he recounted, betraying his paranoia about the medical establishment. "They did not like that, none of them. I said, 'I'll call you if I die.'"

While I was amused by the image of my still-rebellious dad fighting with his doctors from beyond the grave, I was also—obviously—disturbed by the idea of his demise. And though I didn't mention it, lest I wound his pride, I knew there was one glaringly obvious medical opinion my dad had no choice but to accept: He could never go back into the swamp again.

Looking back on our trip, I felt as though I should have recognized my dad's struggles on the trail as a sign of having been more than just the fatigue that came with age. My dad's body had gone through more than just your usual wear and tear; he'd spent decades subjecting it to outright abuse. In my haste to rebuild a relationship with him, I had pushed him past his limits. Now it looked as if he had lost any chance of doing the thing he loved most for the rest of his life—and it was all my fault. And for what? We had seen only two snakes. By that measure, his last trip into the swamp had been a total failure.

"Anyway," his e-mail concluded, as though he was

writing to a business associate and not a blood relative, "it would be wrong of me not to tell you."

Whenever I talk to people about my dad's eccentricities, they either dismiss his behavior as faintly quirky and move on to the next topic, or they claim to have parents who are just as weird themselves. "My dad wears sweaters with reindeer on them!" they'll tell me. Or, "My dad has a much-younger girlfriend, too." Inevitably, these so-called eccentric parents prove to be the type who own summer homes or are retired from a career as a partner in a law firm or as a college professor. Some have weird hobbies, like collecting milk jugs, or have chemical dependencies, but they appear normal in every other way. Some just have highly unpleasant personalities, but a jerk does not a weirdo make.

My now-wife, Megan, never said such things while we were dating. This is probably because her own family is as normal as they come, so she is both shocked by my dad's weirdness and knows that nothing in her own family background could possibly compete with it—which is strange, given that they are prolifically Catholic, and there are so many of them. Her parents met in high school and are still happily married. Her father retired early from the government job he had held steadily since graduating from college because it had good benefits and he knew it would eventually net him a stable pension; he is now an independent consultant for a government contracting firm. Her mother retired recently from her job as a teacher of special-needs children; she volunteers at a local library. They still live in the large, clean house in the suburbs where Megan and her siblings grew up. The weirdest thing her dad ever does is thoughtfully but somewhat obsessively send his three kids travel briefs from the State Department when one of them plans to visit a foreign country, or maybe forward along a few too many safety warnings about recalled products. In other words, he's not abnormal in any way.

Maybe this is why things worked out so well between us in the first year we were dating. Opposites attract and all, plus she had provided exactly the right kind of sounding board for me as I sorted out all of the issues surrounding my dad, our trip, and his health. Once I had returned from the swamp, we had agreed she would move into my place, and in the early fall, she and her amazing cat, George, had done just that. The memories of my time in the swamp with my dad receded from my brain.

But come October, months after my dad had made his announcement about his health problems, his heart was off-rhythm. This was a symptom he hadn't experienced during previous heart problems. In 1989, he'd had a minor heart attack; in the mid-1990s, he had been hospitalized for shortness of breath and chest pains. Both times he had refused a recommended pacemaker. Then, in 2004, he had been diagnosed with congestive heart failure after becoming severely bloated and weak, a problem made worse when he had waited too long to get treatment. I had found about each of these incidents well after the fact, which hadn't been too surprising, given that my dad's approach to his health has always been defined by hiding—hiding from concerned family members, hiding from doctors, and especially, at that time, hiding from the bills he couldn't afford as a broke, mostly uninsured person.

Now my dad was hoping that a new doctor would run a fresh set of tests and diagnose him differently. He desperately wanted someone to tell him that his condition could be managed with medication and "taking it easy" rather than surgery and devices. He wanted to erase his medical history and start over. But the new doctor, as was accepted professional procedure, insisted on seeing the existing medical chart and came to the same conclusion that my dad had heard in July: He needed the defibrillator implant as soon as possible.

"He was simply a salesman," wrote my dad a few weeks after this second diagnosis. When he refused to even consider the procedure, "I was told that if my heart rhythm becomes irregular with pain in the future to cough hard."

He went on to explain his deep suspicions that the whole business was just another capitalistic scheme by the greedy medical industry. "I know this: I now have VT, which I did not have before. It's obvious that when conglomerated doctors and health care monopolies don't have a patient who only needs routine monitoring, they make the 'patient' have the conditions through stress tests and/or other means, and thus be in need of expensive, lucrative operations and prescription medications," he expounded. "The fast-track treadmill 'test' is their procedure of choice to putcha just where they want you."

My dad had always been a little paranoid.

But maybe that was just his way of defending himself against the frightening truth about the inevitable health problems that had come with aging. Or at least the inevitable health problems that come with aging after spending fifty years abusing your body. But if he had his coping mechanism, what about mine? I had almost lost my dad, just when we had (barely) started to reconnect. And now he was refusing to follow the medical advice that could preserve his life. What would happen if, next time, he didn't recover?

My dad would want to be remembered as a consummate rebel, a guy who fought the establishment to the bitter end. He would want to be thought of as a lifelong protector of the environment and underdogs. He would want his sons to say that he was a pretty cool guy, though even he'd admit that he didn't deserve to be called a good father. The grim reality was that the sum total of his accomplishments barely amount to anything, and that we'll remember him as a highly intelligent man who had wasted his talent, and a stubborn mule who imperiled his health by insisting that his doctors were conspiring against him. But we will also remember him as a pretty interesting guy: an amiable interlocutor in sports chat, a worthy opponent in board games, and someone who had a reliably healthy sense of humor about himself. It could be worse.

If I were to lose my dad, one thing was clear: I would remember our snake expedition as a failure. Leaving the area a day early due to my dad's lack of stamina and my lack of dedication to the whole enterprise was a nagging disappointment. We had left behind some unfinished business. Our goal had been to observe a thriving copperbelly population in the wild. For one reason or another, it hadn't happened.

In the summer of 2006, I was in a car headed from Detroit to Grand Rapids with my dad and my brother Matt after a Tigers game. Matt and I ganged up on my dad for one reason or another, and after the double-barrel attack from his sons, my dad played the hurt card by impersonating the dramatic narrator of a nature show. "The old lion, rejected from his pride," he moaned. "What will become of him?"

By suggesting the swamp trip the following year, I had shown that I wasn't rejecting him—that in fact I wanted to find out what he was all about. But I hadn't embraced what he had spent so much of his life doing in the way he had probably hoped I would. I spent barely any time researching or preparing for the trip. I didn't go into the water with him. I made too big of a deal out of the bugs. I complained about being outdoors at every opportunity. As much as I, like my dad, wanted the snakes' habitat to be protected, I still thought they were kind of gross. Unlike him, I actually wanted to go home, and, if I'm being honest, I secretly celebrated his fatigue because it meant I'd be granted a reprieve.

And yet the guilt I felt over my craven inability to man up was incredibly easy to ignore during the Brooklyn winter. Megan moved in, I started a demanding new writing job, and my dad and I communicated regularly enough about other things. Who had the failure hurt, really? My life was humming along, as well as it ever had, and my only encounters with nature came when I needed to take a shortcut across the park, which is to say, almost never.

But then a funny thing happened. My dad had described to me how he felt the call of the swamp every spring, just as the snakes were coming out of hibernation, and I had laughed at the improbability and absurdity of it in the same way that I would ridicule a friend who tells me I should really try yoga. But as March headed into April, it occured to me that it had been one year since my dad and I had decided to go on our trip. And soon after, I was surprised to find that my mind had immovably set itself on going back into the swamp.

Bizarrely, the need to go back had little to do with not having accomplished our mission the year before. It mainly arose out of an unlikely sense that snake hunting was our "thing"—a belated one, sure, but my dad and I would always have Hillsdale. But I also knew that someone needed to go back as my dad's proxy, because he couldn't. My dad's annual checkup on the snake population could only be done now via drive-by; he might as well stay home and check it out on Google Earth. With no other volunteers making themselves known, it was up to me to be his stand-in.

When I informed my dad of this unexpected revelation, he was nothing short of ecstatic, exclaiming that I, too, must have had an awakening and heard the "call of the wild." He went as far as to call me "Swamp Thang." So it was decided: In early May, I would go back into the swamp by myself—but not entirely alone. My dad wouldn't be trekking next to me—asking him to do that would have been asking him to risk his life—but he would come to Hillsdale County with me, where he would help me navigate the swamps from the comfort of his car, via walkie-talkie. Best of all, he would prepare me, and I promised to listen this time.

I'm not exactly sure why I hadn't heeded any of my dad's preparation advice for our initial foray, but I'm sure it had had something to do with exactly how far taking my dad's advice had gotten me in my life up to that point, which was nowhere. In order to trust him in preparation for this solo expedition, I had a lot of skepticism to shed. The last time my dad and I had been earnest preparation partners was during my quest for glory in the fifth-grade spelling bee. It didn't exactly go well.

It should be immediately disclosed that my fifth-grade teacher's name was Mrs. Imogene Vader. This poor woman. She was probably sixty years old, had birch-tree white hair, and at the parent-teacher conference, told my mom, "John doesn't listen much in class, but he can do the Rubik's Cube faster than anyone at school." How weird it must have been for her to have lived fifty-plus years as kindly Mrs. Vader, happily married to the even more cursed Mr. Vader, and then, suddenly, with the release of *Star Wars* in 1977, become known—at least to many of her students—as the Dark Lord of the Sith, Darth Vader.

Obviously this provided my friends and me with hours of enjoyment. Out of her earshot, we frequently employed Darth Vader's husky helmet breathing. In art class one day, I composed bloody light-saber battle stories between Mrs. Vader and various television characters, most notably Crazy Cooter from *The Dukes of Hazzard*. At home, my mom helped me pretend that Mrs. Imogene Vader was actually the patient mother of Darth Vader. I played the part of Darth, defiant schoolboy with a distaste for hot breakfast cereal.

Mom: *Eat your Cream of Wheat, Darth! It's good for you!*

Darth: *Don't be too proud of this technological terror you've constructed!*

Mom: *How was school, Darth?*
Darth: *When I left you, I was but the learner. Now I
    am the master!*

Once Mrs. Vader gave me the nod to go to the school-wide
spelling bee, I immediately learned that getting into one of
those was the worst thing that could have possibly happened
to me. It instantly doubled my homework. I was given
a small booklet with a list of all of the words that might
come up during the competition. The first night, my dad
led my brother and me in an impromptu spelling quiz, but
by the next night he'd dropped his insistence that I study,
and I ignored studying words in favor of flipping through
my baseball card collection. My ten-year-old logic: If I could
correctly spell the name of St. Louis Cardinals reliever Al
"the Mad Hungarian" Hrabosky, then I could handle pretty
much any word during the spelling bee. The night before the
spelling bee, though, I was filled with dread. And my dad
made it worse. Every time he started to quiz me on spelling
words, he would eventually drift off into a story about his
school days, which always seemed to concern evading the
neighborhood bully or showing bigger kids his prowess at
baseball.

The next day came and I wanted to throw up. The entire fifth grade was filed not into the spacious gymnasium
but into a claustrophobic room used mainly for orchestra
practice. There were 150 students and grown-ups occupying
a space designed for forty. Kids were sitting on radiators,
window sills, each other. It was a zoo. Worse, my dad,
who was an unemployed graduate student at the time, had

actually shown up, meaning that I was responsible for the reputations of two members of the Sellers family.

I sat in a folding chair alongside the other seven competitors, acting as if I hadn't a care in the world. I crossed my legs, which were encased in some gaudy red-black-and-yellow-plaid wool flannel pants my mom had decided I looked good in. Inside my head, though, the feeling was that of gravy being sucked into a black hole. My dad gave me the "V" sign. At the time, I had no idea what that meant.

Mrs. Yared, our zaftig music teacher, read out the words. A panel of her peers, including Mrs. Vader, were judging us. I would have felt better if my pants weren't so damn itchy. I scratched my legs and waited for my turn to spell. Some poor schlub misspelled an easy word that I didn't hear, and he walked to a seat in the front row that had been set aside for eliminated contestants. His face was beet red.

My word was "piano." I couldn't believe my luck. The word was so easy; it was nowhere near as difficult as the inconceivably long words my dad had been quizzing me on. Not to mention, I had been taking piano lessons for three years. To prove how utterly beneath me this word was, I spat out "P-A-I-N-O!" Mrs. Yared, her bulbous head tilted to one side, asked, "Can you spell that again, John? "P-A-I-N-O," I said, this time incredibly aware that I was about to become the class punching bag. My pants itched. Mrs. Yared flashed me a look that equated to: "You have no musical talent and now you can't even spell 'piano'? Get thee hence!" I left the stage, looking straight at the kid who was disqualified first, who was stifling a laugh.

Perhaps even he was aware that "paino" does not have a definition, has no alternate spellings or pronunciations, does not have a language of origin. Yet it could be used in a sentence, as the class clown knew all too well when he yelled, spawning a brief class-wide catchphrase in the process: "Paino—what a dork!"

Even my dad laughed. I wanted to say, "Paino attention to the kid in the plaid flannel pants," but I knew it would do no good. Eventually my classmates stopped calling me "Paino" and resumed bugging me to solve their Rubik's Cubes. I never truly recovered socially, though, and after the year ended, I switched to a different school and quickly lost touch with my friends in the class. In the sixth-grade spelling bee, I was removed after misspelling the word "toehold" "T-O-W-H-O-L-D." That was a homophone, though, and didn't make a very good nickname.

When I reminded my dad of this disaster, he said that he remembered my being incredibly nervous and suspected that my subconscious had blown it for me because it wanted me to get off the stage. "That's possible," I said. Either way, I spelled "piano" wrong. My dad and I agreed that he'd be a better coach this time around.

TEN

The next six weeks consisted of a flurry of preparation. I realized I hadn't taken the first trip seriously at all. I had physically gone on the expedition with my dad, but I had treated the whole thing more like watching a nature show: I had observed, not participated. This time, I knew more was at stake. My dad wouldn't be going into the swamp, so the success or failure of the mission rested entirely on my shoulders. To do this right, I'd have to listen carefully to everything he told me. I'd have to take him seriously.

My dad gave me a long list of equipment I'd need, some of which I could borrow from him. The required items included boots that were waterproof up to the ankle, dark-colored clothing, durable socks, and gardening gloves. Considering that on our last trip I'd been dressed like a clown, this new gear was going to be a significant change. While New York City isn't known for its selection of outdoor adventure equipment, I was able to find a specialty store near the Financial District that was literally crammed with gear and staffed by knowledgeable salespeople who helped me make appropriate selections. I cringed as I looked at the price tags; what were the odds that I'd ever end up using this stuff again? I comforted myself with thoughts of future eBay auctions as I took out my credit card.

I also had the novel idea that I should do a little snake research of my own. My dad had tried to teach me everything he knew, but I was never sure if what he told me was apocryphal, and I figured that since I would be venturing into the swamp on my own, I should have a more well-rounded knowledge of what I would be dealing with. And so I bought books that would help me recognize snakes visually, I bought scientific books about snakes, and then I branched out into literary collections of stories about snakes and wilderness adventures. I even set my DVR to record any program with the word "snake" in its title or description. In the course of this research, I discovered there were people who actually made fairly stable careers out of their obsessions with snakes and nature. A professor at Cornell University, Dr. Harry W. Greene, the same age as my dad, has penned multiple books about snakes and channeled his reptilian enthusiasm into scholarly erudition. Another snake enthusiast, Lee Grismer, hosted a show about his searches for reptiles on the Discovery Channel; he was even accompanied by a son, Jesse, who was equally passionate about scaly beasts and clearly respected his father's work. Finding out about these men underscored for me what I'd always known: The snakes were far from the most eccentric thing about my dad.

My research also confirmed what my dad had always told me: The copperbelly snake is sadly overlooked, even among people who love snakes. Because they're by no means the biggest or baddest snakes in the animal kingdom, or even the continental United States, they are understudied and uncelebrated; few mentions of them could be found in any of the literature I'd picked up. In a way, this made my job more interesting, because I'd always delighted in championing the unknown and obscure, from indie bands to uncool games. But it also meant my job was more important, because no one else was looking out for these snakes.

The information I'd accumulated in preparation for the trip had made a would-be snake obsessive out of me by the time I was packing up to leave. The night before my flight to Grand Rapids, where I planned to spend a day visiting my mom before setting off on the two-day excursion my dad had planned for us, I rattled off snake statistics to Megan as though I was talking about the lineup of the Detroit Tigers.

"Did you know that copperbellies can live up to thirty years?" I asked. I pictured a copperbelly snake with a goatee, beginning to fret about career advancement.

"What's a copperbelly again?" she replied inattentively. "Is that some kind of microbrew from Oregon?" I began to understand how my dad must have felt. It's tough to find a receptive audience for tidbits of snake knowledge.

"It's the kind of snake I'm going to look for," I explained. "The snake my dad is obsessed with."

"I know," she admitted. "That was just my way of saying that I think you're crazy."

"Aha," I said, and began to consider that it might be true.

◆ ◆ ◆

The next day, my mom picked me up at Gerald R. Ford International Airport in Grand Rapids (the "international" part refers solely to Canada). Even though my parents were a poor match to begin with and had been divorced for more than twenty-five years, they still lived within fifteen miles of each other. While it was easy to see my dad's reasons for staying near Grand Rapids—it's fairly affordable, it offered him easy access to the nature he loved to be around, and it was miles away from the stifling, well-to-do world he grew up in and couldn't wait to escape—my mom's reasons for staying here now that she was retired were harder to grasp. Grand Rapids has never been a hotbed for theater, museums, and the other cultural pursuits my mom enjoys, and it seems she would have much better access to these sorts of things two hours away in Ann Arbor. When I brought this up to her, she joked that she had to remain in her house because "my kitties love it in the sunroom."

After a restful evening involving my mom's delicious homemade lasagna and some equally gluttonous channel flipping, I awoke the next morning to the sound of pouring rain. As if on cue, my cell phone buzzed and the caller ID read DAD.

"Greetings, sir," he said. "If you don't want to go, that's okay with me."

"What are you talking about?" I asked, knowing that while he was referring overtly to the weather, his true intent was to gauge how serious I was about going to Hillsdale. "When should I come by?"

Satisfied by my level of commitment, he admitted, "The

snakes aren't going to be out today. They don't like the rain. Sunny day on the forecast tomorrow, though."

I of course was relieved that I wouldn't have to go into the swamp for another day, but more than anything I was relieved that my dad was the one to call off the trip, and for reasons that no one could argue with. Plus, I got to spend another day eating my mom's home cooking and watching carefree TV. I suggested that we restructure our plan as a day trip for the following morning and told him that, rain or shine, I would be showing up at his place bright and early in the morning.

"Looking forward to it," he said. "I've got the walkies." He was referring not to an unfortunate medical condition but to the set of walkie-talkies we had discussed using so he might help me to navigate through uncertain cell phone service. Trekking through the wilderness using walkie-talkies is something that I couldn't help but find kick-ass. Also cool: Because of the rain, what would have been a leisurely two-day jaunt would become a fast-paced race against the clock. If I didn't find what I was looking for in the small window of time I would have, I would fail—again. It would make the excursion more like a game of skill. I'd like to think I do my best work under pressure. Would that turn out to be true?

The next morning, with the rain having given way to the clear, pleasant skies that are typical of early May in Michigan, my dad emerged from his house on the rural out-skirts of Grand Rapids with binoculars around his neck and dressed in fairly ordinary clothes. No country camos this time, since he wouldn't be doing any "heavy swamping." He looked just as healthy—or unhealthy—as he had when we'd set off together the first time, almost a year ago. We packed up my dad's car, mixing my newly purchased wilderness gear with his heavily used stuff, and we set off on the two-and-a-half-hour drive south into Hillsdale County.

In so many ways, the return to Hillsdale would be harder than my first trip here. I knew what I was getting into, in terms of terrain, but there were more unknowns. Would I get lost? Would I be able to tolerate standing knee-deep in water? Would I see a snake? Would I figure out how to operate the confounded walkie-talkie? Whatever happened, there would be no one right next to me to guide me through it—or to entertain me, except via wireless. I was going to be alone.

Turning onto Cellars Road, my stomach began to flutter. I felt like my dad was driving me to take the SATs. I no longer wanted to do this. I wasn't going to back out now, but I really didn't want this anymore. I had taken my dad's presence for granted the last time we'd been here; this time, I really felt like I needed him. I couldn't fathom how I would pull this off without him.

Thoughts of everything that could possibly go wrong were flooding my brain. "Dad, what about leeches?" I asked, remembering the leech scene from *Stand by Me*. I had no interest in getting into that situation. "How do I avoid them?"

"I've only gotten leeches on me twice," he said. "That's only two occasions out of many, many times walking in swamps, so it's highly unlikely." His determination for me to succeed boosted my confidence, but I still envisioned riding home covered with slimy bloodsuckers.

Once we reached the cabin, we took a quick walk around the lake. The footpath here was easily navigable, so it was manageable for my dad, despite his condition. The good news was that it was much cooler this time around. I was pleased to note that there were virtually no bugs, and a nice wind made our stroll around the lake a breeze, literally. Next, we decided to check out the smaller swamp behind the house, something my dad claimed he would still be okay to do with me, as long as we went slowly, since the walk there wouldn't require him to do much more than move down a slight incline. We overshot the entry into the easily walkable underbrush that surrounded the swamp, so I ran up a hill that we suspected was separating us from the swamp area in an effort to help us get our bearings. Before I left, I told my dad to sit on a fallen tree and wait for me to get back, but even as I began my ascent, I saw that curiosity was getting the better of him. He raked the underbrush with his walking stick, presumably checking for wandering snakes. I ran up the steep hill and clambered over a fence that must have cordoned off the back of the property, and reached the top of a ridge. I still didn't see the swamp we were looking for, just hundreds and hundreds of yards of small plants, fallen branches, and tall, light-obscuring trees, covering the forest floor. It was an impressive sight, the kind of thing a city dweller rarely gets to see, but as my dad might say, time was a-wastin'. I hastened back to where I had left my dad less than ten minutes ago, but when I returned, there was no sign of him anywhere.

How had I ever allowed him to come out here? I should have known that he would push himself, against better judgment—if he even had better judgment. I worried that he'd had another heart attack, and I pictured him lying unconscious somewhere in the dense underbrush. I searched for him frantically, looking everywhere I could think. I retraced our steps back to the lake. I went back to the cabin. I walked all the way back to the car, which was parked on the road outside the cabin gate. When I didn't find him, I walked back to where I had last seen him, but of course, he still wasn't there. After a half hour of searching in vain, I noticed a footprint in the mud, and I realized that I knew where he was.

My dad must have found his way to the swamp, and now I would have to attempt to follow his trail to sniff it out for myself. Everything looked familiar, yet totally foreign—it was easy to understand why the woods can be disorienting. Luckily, it only took me a few minutes to find my way. We hadn't been far from the swamp at all. When I reached the small swamp, I saw my dad standing on the other side, talking to himself as though nothing had happened. No "sorry I wandered off on you, John" was in order as far as he was concerned.

"Dad!" I called out. "Where the hell were you?"

"I've been here. Took you longer than I thought it would to find me," he said, as if we were playing hide-and-seek. I chastised him for being so cavalier about his health and told him he'd better not wander off again without telling me first.

He said he was concerned about the low water level in the swamp, especially considering that it had just rained and there had been a lot of snow over the winter. The absence of copperbellies here was still a mystery, but he did note that their migration patterns can change from year to year within a particular ecosystem. He suggested that they might be clustering in the heavier swamp area this spring.

We trudged back to the car. Last year, we had walked down Cellars Road to get to the heavier swamps by using the portion of the street that had been closed to cars. This year, because walking such a distance would have put too much strain on my dad's heart, we drove around three sides of a square to reach the far side of the closed road, which was nearer to the entry point for the heavy swamps. Near a DEAD END sign, my dad pulled the Outback to the side of the road and turned off the engine. The moment I'd been dreading had come. It was time for me to go into the swamp alone.

It was already one p.m., so I only had a small window of daylight left. Based on my experience from the previous year, I was going to need every one of those hours if I was going to have any hope of getting this done. Still, I wasn't quite ready. I needed a last-minute refresher course. As we sat in the parked car, my dad gave me some tips while we ate sandwiches. He was taking huge bites, with his shockingly authentic-looking new set of fake teeth, chomping quickly and making messy chewing noises.

"We know two things," he said between bites. "They gotta mate. And they gotta eat."

While I knew he wasn't content to live vicariously through me, he was happy that one of his sons had taken an interest in what he did for a living. He continued giving basic snake-spotting pointers and drew a rudimentary map of the area we had visited last summer. There were lines and circles saying "swamp" and "opening" and "stump." He then placed an X at the far end of the mark indicating "swamp" and drew a hash mark. "If I sit on that sitting log, by and by I'll see one," he said, referring to the mark. "Just look for anything that looks like a bicycle tire," he suggested, describing the look of a copperbelly's skin.

The material he was covering sounded more advanced than what I was ready for. I wanted to find a snake, but my bigger concerns were more in the realm of what it was like to walk in the swamp water. The prospect of wading into murky liquid was mildly terrifying to me, and had been since I was a little kid. This no doubt had everything to do with my dad thinking, in 1975, that it would be a good idea to take Mark and me to the theater to see *Jaws*. My five-year-old brain quickly recognized that whenever the ominous shark music kicked in, I needed to haul ass to the lobby to avoid seeing the carnage. The thought that there might be something sinister lurking beneath the surface of the water had been difficult to overcome my entire life—I thought about it even when I was in a public swimming pool. Even though my dad had already said that I was unlikely to encounter any leeches, who knew what else might be in there?

Beyond that, though, was my general distaste for ickiness. And swamp water, in which mosquitoes breed, reptiles and fish release waste, and bacteria festers, was nothing if not icky. The prospect of slipping and falling into that soupy mess utterly disturbed me.

"The only thing that's tricky to me is logs that are down beneath the water," said my dad. "Submergent vegetation and logs are the dangers, but the bottom is solid. The boots you got on are going to carry you through—until you get above the ankle."

"Wait a second," I gasped. Stupidly, perhaps, I figured that a pair of two-hundred-dollar shoes labeled as being waterproof would protect my feet from any kind of interaction with the water. I pictured all kinds of scary swamp critters swimming inside my boots. "What happens when I get above the ankle?" I asked. "That'll happen pretty quickly!"

"Then your feet will get wet."

"Why would anyone ever want to do this, then?" My dad knew my question was rhetorical. I *was* going to do this. I *had* to do this. I was just going to hate every second of it, or at least that was my prediction while sitting in the Outback.

He returned to telling me how to approach a snake if I happened to see one. "You gotta do the human sloth," he explained, pantomiming a slow, silent creeping movement that made him look a little zombie-like. "As long as you do the sloth, you won't spook 'em. It's a matter of getting my feet as close to the snake as possible first. And then I go for the biggest mass of coil."

Now, it should be said that my dad hadn't physically caught a snake since 1995, which not coincidentally had followed the radio-tracking incident that had accidentally killed a pregnant snake. After that had happened, my dad, who had previously loved to catch all snakes he found in the wild before releasing them back into their habitat, had come to believe that snakes just needed to be left alone. That this might have suggested some over-identification with snakes on his part wasn't even lost on him. But I felt a vague sense that my solo swamp debut would not matter unless I actually caught a snake. I felt a need to return to Brooklyn being able to say, "Yeah, I've caught a snake." I realized this was probably the world's most ridiculous reason to try to catch a snake. But given what I knew about the way masculinity was judged, I wouldn't have been surprised if it was also the most common.

My mission was to find healthy adult copperbellies and report my findings back to my dad, but if I actually decided to follow through on this snake-catching scheme, I wanted to know what I would be up against. I asked my dad what I really needed to know: "How quickly will they bite you?"

"Sometimes they don't," he said. "Usually, though, it's right away. So if you can, go for the body. The body is most of the animal. They move with their heads first and tend to bite at the point of contact."

Then I remembered something disgusting my dad had once told me. "Won't they urinate on me?"

"Oh, I forgot about that," he said, chuckling. "That's their stink mechanism. Happens as soon as the tail comes out of the water. If they writhe, you'll get sprayed everywhere." He paused, and a curious look passed over his face. "I actually have come to like the smell, but that's just me."

My dad had just told me he liked the smell of snake urine. I was about to wander into a swamp alone, and I was taking instructions from a person who was clearly insane. With that, I exited the car, clutching my walkie-talkie for dear life, and entered the brush.

ELEVEN

The strategy I chose to adopt for the first part of the hike, which would take me through a dry, dense forest and over a hill to the large backwoods swamp into which my dad had waded on our other trip, was to get it over with as quickly as possible. I could do this now that I was free from the burden of having to wait for my dad, which was the only upside of making this hike without him. My rationale was that the faster I walked, the sooner it would be over, the sooner I'd be back at home watching TV and eating nachos. Beyond that, I just wanted to get there before I had time to think about what was about to happen.

Even though I was following my dad's rudimentary hand-drawn map, and I began to remember where I needed to go, I started to worry that I was on the wrong path. It wouldn't have been the first time that had happened to me. Once, while traveling alone in Italy, my limited knowledge of the local language, coupled with a biologically determined tendency never to ask for directions, led to a travel mishap of epic proportions. I thought I had hopped a train headed for Rome, but as it turned out I was bound for the exact opposite direction, and I was left with no choice but to disembark in a desolate port town in the middle of the night. I walked around the empty streets, lit only by flickering fluorescent bulbs, wondering if the population of the town had been decimated by an epidemic. I was scared. No one knew where I was. It might have taken days for someone to notice that I'd gone missing, more than enough time for a sadistic Italian butcher to kidnap me and use me as a whetstone for his meat cleavers. At nearly one in the morning, I found a café that was miraculously still open, and just before six, I boarded a train bound, finally, for Rome.

In retrospect, getting lost had been a positive experience, in that I'd learned how to be alone in a strange place. Although two places could hardly be as different as coastal Italy and rural Michigan, I suspected the lessons I'd absorbed on that misadventure would serve me well here. At least I'd know whether or not I was being chased by butchers.

So as I ventured from point A (the Subaru) to point B (the swamp), I walked quickly and without emotion. I pretended I was a soldier in a particularly uneventful war, and said "hut hut hut" to myself like a backwoods drill sergeant. Within minutes, I had reached the open field on a hill I remembered from last time, and it was filled with sunlight and wild daisies in bloom. It was hot in the afternoon sun, but, again, at least this time there weren't any bugs. I passed over the hill and chanced upon a family of pheasants, which initially startled me, but then I laughed because the word always makes me think of peasants. I would have been even more startled if I'd come across a family of peasants. In any case, I really wished I had been looking for pheasants instead of copperbelly snakes, because then I'd be done.

I reached the impenetrable wall of brambles at the other side of the field. This was all that was left to separate me from the swamp. Through the thick tangle of vines and branches, I could even see the murky water that awaited me. And I didn't like it. I took a moment to wipe my forehead on the sleeve of my shirt and took a swig out of my canteen. Drawing a deep, nervous breath, I used my walking stick to clear a path through the thorny obstacle in front of me, and a few slow minutes later, emerged on the other side.

I pulled my walkie-talkie out of my pack and radioed my dad to let him know I'd arrived at the swamp. He said, "Boom. You made good time, suh."

"I wanted to get it over with. I basically ran here," I explained. "Saw some pheasants, though."

"Nature is all around you. Enjoy."

I walked around the perimeter of the swamp for twenty minutes, hoping that I'd just randomly come across a colony of snakes so that I wouldn't have to go into the swamp itself. Essentially, I was procrastinating, which was something I knew how to do well, as any of the commissioners of my fantasy baseball league could tell you. But no snakes were presenting themselves to me, so I was going to have to get my feet wet.

I consulted my dad's chicken-scratch map again and used it to find the log he had described to me earlier. Covered in moss and about three feet high, it actually looked like a comfortable place to sit, threat of termites and beetles not-withstanding. I sat down and was happy to find that it was as accommodating as I thought it might be, although it was damper than I would have preferred. While I'd take an afternoon in a dark bar with a cold beer in front of me over this any day, as I sat on the log on a sunny, bug-free day, I saw the pleasant side to being outdoors, even if it was an appeal that came with a time limit. I looked into the water, keeping my eyes peeled for anything that moved. After five minutes, I hadn't seen as much as a dragonfly buzzing on the surface. My dad had explained that the snakes liked to bask in the sun on the branches in the middle of the swamp, far from where I was sitting. So I began to formulate a plan to get out there.

Arrows on my dad's map indicated his favorite entry point. I stood up, mustering my dwindling resolve, and walked quickly to where he said I'd be able to wade out into the open water most easily. I radioed my dad and said, "Wish I had better news. I haven't seen any snakes yet."

"Where are you now?" he asked, with concern.

"I sat on the log you pointed out and nothing swam by."

"Ah. You're going to have to get in the water to find them."

"Tell me about it."

I tightened my laces and took my first step into the water. At this point, I was getting worried that I wasn't going to see any snakes at all, and that all the preparation and exertion would have been in vain. My dad had sounded understandably nervous when I told him I hadn't seen anything yet. I hoped it was the case that I just didn't have "good eyes" today, instead of the scarier prospect that this area's copperbelly population had been wiped out. With luck, wading out to the center of the swamp would at least help me figure out which of those possibilities was actually true. It was something I knew I needed to do not just for my dad, but for myself.

There was a distinct sucking feeling when I took my first step into the swamp, which was immediately followed by a rush of panic. The paranoia began: What's floating in there? What might bite me? But once my foot adjusted to the squishy quality of the muck, I saw that standing in a few inches of water wasn't as bad as I'd imagined for so long—at the very least, the waterproof boots were doing their job. I proceeded slowly forward, taking small, tentative steps, scanning the water in front of me for fallen branches or other hurdles. With my fifth step, however, I was deep enough that the water level had reached the ankle line of my boot, and suddenly my socks had been drowned by painfully cold swamp liquid. The vacuum inside my shoes had been broken. After a lifetime spent avoiding it, the swamp had finally claimed me.

I walked around incredibly slowly, almost as if I was groping through a room in the dark; I was more focused on not tripping over a submerged log than on spotting a snake, or on keeping quiet so that I'd actually have a chance of spotting one. The water was getting higher and higher up my legs, up to the shin, and then to the knee. The whole time I was nearly gagging out of disgust, making "ew" sounds like a third grader forced to eat lima beans. The water in this part, out of the sunlight, was chilly. It was also a murky brown. And it smelled a bit like dishwater. It was as if I were walking around in a giant sink in the aftermath of an especially lively dinner party thrown by herpetologists.

Up ahead of me lay the open water, the only part of the swamp that was exposed to unbroken sunlight. It was also the scariest part of the swamp, in my estimation, because I knew from watching my dad wade out there that it was where the water was deepest. My dad had been up to his waist in swamp water there on our earlier trip. I was apprehensive to get in that deep, since once I couldn't see my feet anymore, I feared the worst would happen. I decided to hold off on attempting that for as long as I could and walked along the edges of the swamp, thigh-deep, slowly, looking for my elusive quarry. As far as I could see, there was no sign of life.

I stood in the swamp, acting casual, trying to get used to the feeling of being thigh-deep in uncertain water. I tried rocking back and forth with my hands in my pockets, as if I was waiting for my train to show up. "This isn't so bad," I said out loud. "I *like* swamp water." Then an inspired idea hit me: I took out my cell phone to see if there was service. There was! Last year there was not—kudos to Verizon! So I decided to surprise Megan, who was at work in Manhattan, with what was assuredly the first phone call she had ever received from a swamp. Even standing in two feet of stagnant water, I was pretty excited to bestow this distinction upon her. Although naturally, I played it cool.

"What's up?" I asked when she picked up the line.

"Nothing. Working. What's wrong with the reception? There's an echo."

"Oh. Well, I'm standing in the middle of a swamp, that's all." I added a confident sniff to indicate that I was pretty pleased with myself.

"Gross," she said. "Have you seen any snakes at least?"

"Actually, no. There's still one more place I need to check, but I haven't seen any. I might just decide to call it a day and admit I'm a failure."

"You know you're not a failure, but I bet you don't smell very good."

I told her I'd see her soon and started to walk back to dry land. If I couldn't even see snakes from where I was now, I figured, I doubted I'd find any after going through all the trouble of getting out to the open water. I scrambled back to the shore, worried that I was giving up too soon but also thoroughly tired of the whole endeavor. Swamping, I had decided, was just not my thing. Once back on shore, I got my bearings and started to walk back toward the wall of brambles, my socks squishing uncomfortably in my boots. As I took a step forward, I noticed something glinting in the sun off to my left. And I was damned if it didn't look like the rubber of a bicycle tire.

There, resting comfortably on a log not more than twenty feet away from me, was a massive black snake. The glinting, I was happy to discover, was the sunlight shining off its rust-colored underside, confirming that it was indeed one of my dad's beloved copperbellies. My first instinct was to freeze. I didn't want to spook the snake with excessive movement, but I also wanted to document this for my dad. So I fumbled in my backpack for my digital camera and crept closer. Very slowly I snuck up on the snake, snapping photos. I contemplated whether or not I should try to catch it. If I wanted to try, now would be the time to strike. I was less than ten feet away and approaching steadily.

As I got closer, I could see that the snake had noticed me. I was in awe of the fact that it was a healthy, full-grown adult copperbelly, the first one I'd ever seen in the wild, the very kind my dad and I had set out to observe a year ago. Given how long copperbelly snakes can live, it was even possible that my dad had seen this exact snake at some point in the past. Doing the human sloth, I made it to literally five feet from it now. Four. Three. I took a long look, and I watched its forked tongue flick nervously out of its mouth. He definitely saw me. And as I looked back at him, I realized that we understood each other. Or at least I understood the snake: It wanted to be left alone. It wanted to sit there in the sun and enjoy the day. Just by being here, I was ruining it for him. I was ruining this snake's day. The only thing I could do to make amends was to go back to where I had come from.

And just as I reached this conclusion, the same one my dad had reached nearly two decades ago, the snake slid effortlessly into the water. For a split second I thought about diving headlong after it, knowing that my last chance to catch it was at hand. But why? Who would that impress? Certainly not my dad, who would be content to see the photos I had taken, viewing them as reassurance that at least one of his precious copperbellies was healthy and thriving. As it zigzagged away under the black water, seeming not so much afraid of the potential danger I might cause as merely perturbed by my presence, I realized why it was okay that I would never come back to the swamp again. These creatures only wanted to be left alone.

As I left the swamp after a challenging and inspiring and ridiculous day, I radioed my dad to fill him in on all that had transpired.

"Mission accomplished, suh," said my dad, his voice dripping with pride, and not a trace of envy. "Mission accomplished."

I let out a long sigh.

"Relax," he said. "You've made it. You're out of the swamp."

"Forever," I answered, and we both laughed.

EPILOGUE

I could survive prison.

Not because I'm a high-ranking soldier in the Gambino crime family, or because my life has been scratched out on the streets, or even because jujitsu is a friend of mine. The idea of shivs and solitary and bending over for the soap scares me as much as it would any other sniveling whiner who literally screeched the last time he saw a spider crawling out of the bathtub drain. But now that I've waded through a swamp, I'm fairly confident that prison would be a cakewalk.

Okay, so I only stood in water that made it up to my thighs. But come on, leeches were reportedly swimming around in that stuff. I mean, call me overprotective of my reproductive organs, but no way was I going to wade out any deeper and risk having one of those puppies wriggle up any higher.

But we're splitting hairs here. I have stood in a swamp.

Why should it matter if the cold, filthy liquid that seeped into my supposedly waterproof boots, causing my socks to squish revoltingly with every step, totally creeped me out?

I could absolutely survive prison.

Another walk in the woods? Sure, I could endure it—technically. But you'd probably only convince me to risk contracting Lyme disease, stepping in deer droppings, and having panic attacks about homicidal tree people again if armed coercion were involved, or at least a significant cash prize.

My dad, on the other hand, continues to have reveries about trips to Hillsdale in the way that most retirees fantasize about all-inclusive Caribbean cruises. His body hasn't been cooperating, though. Since we returned from our second expedition, his muscular health has further deteriorated; he's at the point now where—and this is mildly shocking, considering that he retains his strident distrust of the medical establishment—he is strongly contemplating surgery for a possible pinched nerve in his neck, as he has been having trouble performing tasks as simple as tying his own shoelaces. Given that he is now seventy, it would seem that the prospects of his venturing through thickets and muck again to check on the copperbellies are growing increasingly dim—at least until either he regains his strength or someone invents a pretty far-out kind of wheelchair, which I sincerely hope is named the Swampinator 5000.

While I am of course very concerned about my dad's health, one unexpected consequence of his assumed incapability of returning to the swamp is that our expeditions to Hillsdale County have necessarily taken on extra meaning.

In my mind, where my childhood memories will always loom large, being with my dad for what might have been his final visit to see his coppers is on par with witnessing Babe Ruth's last game. Sure, my dad's performance wasn't as impressive as it would have been had I tagged along when he was in his prime, but by having been a late convert to the notion of accompanying him into the swamp, I was able to experience the ordeal from an advantageous perspective, that is, as an adult. The additional life experience has allowed me to see him not just as my dad but as something of a peer—one who, like most people, has positive attributes in addition to his (many, many, *many* well-documented) flaws. I have finally come to see his fights to preserve an undersung animal as being entirely admirable.

I'll never look at nature in the unique way that my dad does, but our journeys into the swamp have turned some of my long-held beliefs about wildlife on their ear. It may not sound like much, but every so often, when I'm driving along the highway, I'll catch myself noticing, say, a bird sitting high on a cell-phone tower and chuckle inwardly that I had been thinking to myself, with genuine concern, "I wonder what that little dude is doing up there? I hope he's getting enough to eat!" as if I'd been directly channeling my dad. For a guy whose most telling previous involvements with animal preservation had been through the lyrics of Morrissey, this is a notable improvement. I've even developed the tiniest amount of appreciation for being outdoors. With any luck, the popular recent Internet video of a man orgasmically enjoying the sight of a double rainbow won't offer you a glimpse into my future, but it's no longer impossible for me to consider that such natural wonders might be worth experiencing in person—once in a while.

More than anything, the two swamp excursions with my dad showed me that I could do the hardest thing I could imagine for myself, as long as I was determined and prepared. Am I referring to my decision to enter a swamp to look for snakes? No. I am talking about my bold decision to spend time alone with my dad again after all these years. I would tell him directly that I enjoyed the experience, but he'd just ask me to prove it.

ABOUT THE AUTHOR

JOHN SELLERS is the author of *Perfect From Now On: How Indie Rock Saved My Life* and has written for *GQ, Spin, The Believer,* and *The New York Times,* among many other publications. Originally from Grand Rapids, Michigan, he currently lives in Brooklyn, New York. For more information, visit johnsellers.com.